Edward Frederick Knight

Albania: A Narrative of Recent Travel

Edward Frederick Knight

Albania: A Narrative of Recent Travel

ISBN/EAN: 9783337208875

Printed in Europe, USA, Canada, Australia, Japan

Cover: Foto ©Andreas Hilbeck / pixelio.de

More available books at **www.hansebooks.com**

A SCIENTIFIC FRONTIER.

Page 229.

ALBANIA:

A NARRATIVE OF RECENT TRAVEL.

By E. F. KNIGHT,

BARRISTER-AT-LAW.

WITH ILLUSTRATIONS.

London:
SAMPSON LOW, MARSTON, SEARLE, & RIVINGTON.
CROWN BUILDINGS, 188, FLEET STREET.
1880.

CONTENTS.

CHAPTER I.

Where to go to?—An unknown country—The expedition—Our inventor—Our equipment—The doctor—A useful remedy—The start—Venice—Trieste . . . 1

CHAPTER II.

On board an Austrian Lloyd—Voyage to Spalato—The coast of Istria and Dalmatia—Old Venetian cities—Our fellow-passengers—Pola—A Turkish officer—The Morlaks—Why is England a triangle?—Sebenico—Arrival at Spalato 11

CHAPTER III.

Dalmatian *cuisine*—The Emperor Diocletian—Remains of the old palace—We make two friends—Wines of Dalmatia—Customs of the Morlaks—A visit to Salona—A great fête—Costumes—Morlak singing . 28

CHAPTER IV.

Voyage to Cattaro—A bora—The gulf of Narenta—The Herzegovina—The Island of Curzola—Ragusa—The Bocche di Cattan—The frontier of Montenegro—The fortress of Cattaro—Evening promenade—Personal attractions of the Cattarine ladies—Rough roads—Prince Nikita's coach—Bosnian refugees—A Bosnian's luggage 45

CHAPTER V.

March to Cettinje—The pass across the frontier—Montenegrin warriors—Cettinje—A land of stones—The Prince's Hotel—Frontier disputes—The commission—Montenegrin method of making war—A game of billiards—A Draconic law—A popular prince . . 60

CHAPTER VI.

The occupation of a Montenegrin gentleman—The public library—Prince Nikita's prisoners—Albanian *versus* Montenegrin—A Montenegrin loan—The prince as a sportsman—The museum—The hospital . . . 78

CHAPTER VII.

Journey to Scutari—Atrocities—A runaway—The vale of Rieka—A Montenegrin sailor—The lions of Rieka—The perils of the night 90

CHAPTER VIII.

A great victory—A good old custom—On the Lake of Scutari—The londra—The debateable land—Boat song—Encampment—Scutari—A reminiscence of Cremorne—The brothers Toshli—Willow-pattern plates—At the British consulate 100

CHAPTER IX.

Condition of Albania—Her races—The Mussulman—The Christian—The Arnaut—Prince Scanderbeg—Turkish rule—Albanian language—Gendarmes on strike—A Scutarine beauty—Courtship and marriage—Nuns 116

CONTENTS. vii

CHAPTER X.

PAGE

The bazaar—Turkish gipsies—The vendetta—An assassin—A way to pay debts—Bosnian refugees—A card-party—Paving stones—Burglars—Army doctors—Change for a ten pound note—Our horses . . 132

CHAPTER XI.

Our Lady of Scutari—A miracle—The fête—A funeral—A drunken Arnaut—Our escort—Two more Britons—Warm discussion—War—Marco . . . 151

CHAPTER XII.

March to Podgoritza—An Albanian khan—Our cook—The Fund—Across the lake—Night visitors—The frontier—Podgoritza—The armourer—The war minister—Dobra Pushka 163

CHAPTER XIII.

War preparations—Our camp visitors—An impromptu ball—English-consul fashion—Robbers—Ruins of Douka—A dangerous bath—Bastinado—Karatag yok mir . 181

CHAPTER XIV.

An escort—A Turkish dinner-party—Brigands—Our sportsman—A chief of the league—Objects of the rebels—Achmet Agha—A meeting of the league—The boulim-bashi of Klementi—An Arnaut chieftain 194

CHAPTER XV.

To Gussinje—The valley of the Drin—A rough road—In the mountains—Hospitality—A pretty woman—A scientific frontier—Franciscans—Dog Latin—Marco Milano 215

CHAPTER XVI.

The mission-house — Gropa — The mandolin — A letter from Ali Bey — A trap — Our throats in danger — Retreat — Nik Leka — Proverbs — A pleasant evening . 238

CHAPTER XVII.

Rosso and Effendi — A barbaric feast — Patoulis — Mead — The future of Albania — The Italia Irridenta — Sport in Meriditia — Dick Deadeye 251

CHAPTER XVIII.

The coffin — A Pasha's death — Horse-dealing — The postman — Brigands — An hotel bill — Down the Bojana — Dulcigno — Pirates — Farewell 268

LIST OF ILLUSTRATIONS.

	PAGE
SPALATO	26
BOCCHE DI CATTARO	48
WALLS OF CATTARO	49
CETTINJE	65
THE LONDRA	102
SCUTARI FISHING HARBOUR	109
PODGORITZA	177
A SCIENTIFIC FRONTIER	229

ALBANIA.

CHAPTER I.

Where to go to ?—An unknown country—The expedition—Our inventor—Our equipment—The doctor—A useful remedy—The start—Venice—Trieste.

ONE day last autumn I was sitting in my Temple chambers, wondering what I should do with myself in the Long Vacation, when I was aroused from my reverie by the entrance of my clerk.

"Here is Mr. N., sir."

"Show him in."

N. entered, and his chance visit solved my problem.

"Don't know what to do with yourself? Why, I have the very thing for you. Three friends of mine—Brown, Jones, and Robinson—are preparing for a tour in Albania. I saw Brown this morning, and he told me they wanted somebody else to join their party."

To cut the narrative short, I was introduced to Brown, Jones, and Robinson, as I shall call my travelling companions in this book; and it was not long before I decided to join them in a trip which promised to be a very amusing one. My friends were artists, and had chosen this almost unknown country for their summer tour, as being an unexplored mine for their pencils, both as regards magnificence of scenery and picturesqueness of costume. I myself knew nothing about Albania before starting, with the exception of what I had gleaned from "Childe Harold." The lines where the poet sings,

> Albania, rugged nurse of savage men,

came to my mind; so I took down Byron from my shelves, and read all that he has to say about

> The wild Albanian kirtled to his knee,
> With shawl-girt head, and ornamented gun,
> And gold-embroider'd garments fair to see.

The information was scanty, but sufficient to show me that no more interesting country could have been chosen for our expedition. I purpose, in this book, to give a narrative of our wanderings in Montenegro and Northern Albania.

My aim is not at all an ambitious one, and I do not intend to enter very deeply into the history and already over-discussed politics of the races of Eastern Europe, but merely to jot down my own first rough impressions of the country; for my object is principally to show my readers how well worthy of a visit it is, and by describing the ways and means of travelling in it, to encourage and render some assistance to any who may purpose to follow in our footsteps over the Highlands of ancient Illyria. My fellow-travellers proposed to travel in a rough style, not to hamper themselves with servants, and to ride or walk, as seemed best when we reached the country.

The originator of the expedition, Robinson, had evolved an imaginary Albania from his inner consciousness, and was therefore always ready to answer, off-hand, any question we might ask him as to what we should take with us in the shape of baggage, &c.

He always advanced his opinion so unhesitatingly, and would give us so many facts as to the climate, nature of the country and manners of the people, that, till I knew him better, I imagined that he must have either travelled in these countries himself, or at least have had a very dear and confiding friend who had done so, for no amount of reading could have brought about so intimate an acquaintance with the subject.

We were certain to meet with an abundance of big game, he told us, so must each be provided with a rifle—the result was, I armed myself with a Martini-Henry. He procured a Winchester rifle (I think, later on in our heavy marches, he regretted having taken this ponderous weapon). Brown provided himself with a lighter Winchester carbine. Jones wisely took no rifle with him. We each had a good revolver, and our scanty baggage was contained in three saddle-bags. Robinson, in addition to his other great qualities, was a wonderful inventor, and insisted on furnishing the expedition with a huge tent, which subsequently was christened "the White Elephant." This was packed for the journey in a long coffin-like box, and many were the wranglings and afflictions over that unfortunate package. Cabmen, railway porters, custom-house officers, police, all alike suspected it, and hindered its unhappy progress in every way. A fantastic axe, a gigantic yataghan-looking knife, and a cooking apparatus, were also devised by our ingenious friend, and constructed under his supervision. Many and many a plan he drew up before he perfected these marvellous inventions, and long was it ere he could find artisans intelligent enough to comprehend and carry them out. We trembled for all these *impedimenta*, and warned our friend that four camels at least would be necessary to transport them. Remonstrances were useless; we were told it was impossible to travel in Albania without these; so, with reluctance, and foreboding of future troubles, we gave in. Accidents of various kinds delayed our start. Brown and myself at last waxed impatient, and after waiting long for our tardy companions, who never would come up to the scratch, but postponed the journey from one day to another (each to be fixed and unchangeable), we decided to precede them, and await them either at some Dalmatian port or in Montenegro. We settled to leave London on the 18th of September, took through tickets to Trieste, and appointed to meet in our war-paint at Victoria Station at seven o'clock in the evening, so as to catch the eight o'clock train for the Dieppe boat.

At seven o'clock the whole length of Spiers and Pond's refreshment-bar at Victoria Station was monopolized by the travellers and the numerous friends who had come to see the last of them. "You are certain to have your throat cut, old fellow, so you might just as well have one last beverage with me," was an oft-repeated and encouraging salute.

I should say that those who were spectators of our departure must have imagined that we were bound on an expedition to the centre of Africa, at least. Our appearance was certainly remarkable. We were arrayed in blue flannel shirts, rough blue pilot suits, and top-boots.

Brown, too, had closely shaven his head, which gave him a decided Millbank appearance. Our luggage consisted of a saddle-bag, a rifle, and blanket each. Robinson was anxious for us to take "the White Elephant" with us; we did not see it. I forgot to state that Brown had taken upon himself the charge of the medical department, and had arranged a little box of horrible implements and medicaments. The properties of these I do not think he knew much about. As can easily be imagined, we fought very shy of him in his surgical character throughout the journey. At the last moment we remembered another medicine which might, with advantage, be added to our chest; we had incidentally heard that brandy was a useful remedy in some illnesses. We accordingly sent my clerk over to that excellent tavern, the "Devereux Arms," for a bottle of this fluid; it was lucky we did so, for, curiously enough, both of us suffered on several occasions from those maladies for which it is supposed that beverage is a specific; to such an extent, indeed, that though none of the other bottles in the chest were even uncorked, this one had frequently to be replenished.

In sixty-two hours from the time we left London we were in Venice. We were haunted by two guilty consciences during the whole of our run across Europe. For we had to cross three frontiers, and were laden with contraband, in the shape of revolvers and rifle cartridges. In consequence of our suspicious appearance, our baggage was generally examined. At Modane, where is the most unpleasant frontier custom-house in Europe, the officers have instructions to confiscate all revolvers. Thus we had to conceal our own on our persons. As they were large, and so caused a suspicious-looking protuberance of our outer clothing, we did not feel quite happy until we were again seated in a carriage, and plunged into the darkness of the Mont Cenis.

From Venice we took the steamer to Trieste—a twelve hours' journey. The boat was crowded. Brown and myself tossed up as to whether he or I should sleep alongside a very fat old lady who obstructed the entrance to one of the two only vacant berths. I won the toss, and ungallantly enough surrendered the place of honour to Brown.

At six in the morning we were alongside one of the quays at Trieste, and landed without being subjected to any custom-house inspection. We put up at the Hôtel Delorme, at which well-known hostelry the Prince of Montenegro had been recently staying, on his return from a visit to the Emperor of Austria at Vienna. We found that an Austrian Lloyd steamer started at five the next morning for the different Dalmatian and Albanian ports; so, as Trieste is not a very interesting place, we determined to steam as far as Spalato, and there await our companions. We telegraphed to them to that effect.

We wandered about the town sight-seeing the whole day, visited the Lloyd Arsenal, and called on our consul, Captain Burton, the well-known traveller. He gave us some useful information, and recommended us to several people on the Dalmatian coast. He strongly advised us to take plenty of quinine with us, as the fever season had commenced, and tertians had been exceptionally frequent in Southern Dalmatia this year, after the severe drought this part of Europe had experienced.

We took two *sedea platea* at the Theatre Fenice, the opera for the evening being "Lucia di Lammermoor." The *prima donna* was an English Jewess, Madame Isidore, of whom, as a foreigner, the Triestines seemed to be very jealous, for her excellent singing met with a cold reception. When the opera was concluded, we wandered about the town for a short time. I find in my diary this note: "The beer of Trieste is good."

An English-speaking commissionaire at our hotel had insisted on piloting us about to the different places of interest. He was an amusing man, had tried most professions, had even been a butler in an English family. He had recently been butler, or what here corresponds to a butler, to a Triestine; but, after a few weeks, left his place in disgust, for, as he expressed it, "The Italian no understand life like you English. In cellar no wine. I go to my master. Sar, I leave you."

"Why? what is the reason?"

"Sar, I came here as butler. There is nothing to buttle. I go."

We retired to our beds about one, and enjoyed a few hours' sleep before the time came for embarking.

At three o'clock the next morning we were aroused by our commissionaire, who had promised to see us off. We dressed hastily, and sallied forth in search of an early breakfast before our vessel sailed, and soon found a café which had not yet closed its doors. The waiters, and the place itself, had that disreputable and up-all-night appearance which is only apparent to those who themselves have arisen betimes from sober couches. I think my friend and myself rather regretted that we had so risen, and had not wandered about the town till the hour of sailing; for to turn into bed from one to three is productive rather of discontent with things in general than of that freshness, as of a button, the little cherub proverbially enjoys.

After swallowing our coffee we found our way to our vessel, the "Archduke Paul," bid adieu to our commissionaire, introduced ourselves to the steward, and, selecting two comfortable berths, turned in for a little more sleep.

CHAPTER II.

On board an Austrian Lloyd—Voyage to Spalato—The coast of Istria and Dalmatia—Old Venetian cities—Our fellow-passengers—Pola—A Turkish officer—The Morlaks—Why is England a triangle?—Sebenico—Arrival at Spalato.

WHEN I awoke, the sun was shining brightly through the skylight, and the familiar thud of the screw told me we were under way. On mounting to the deck, I found that we were to have a glorious day to enjoy the scenery of the coast. There was not a cloud in the sky, and a fresh and pleasant breeze was blowing off shore. As our vessel was to touch at nearly every harbour of Istria and Dalmatia, we were never more than one or two miles distant from some coast, either of the continent or of the innumerable islands which stud the Eastern Adriatic from Fiume to Cattaro.

Very few English tourists ever wander among these remote provinces of the Austrian Empire, yet they are exceedingly easy of access, and possibly no countries in Europe are so interesting.

The fine scenery, the picturesque costumes and manners of the population, and above all, the remarkable Roman and Venetian antiquities, render them well worthy of a visit. It is surprising indeed that they are so little known.

The Austrian Lloyd steamers run up and down between Trieste and Corfu three times a week, and are as clean and comfortable as any in the world. Again, all countries under Austrian rule are perfectly secure, banditti being entirely unknown. Of course, if any one ventures inland, one must not expect to meet with all the luxuries of civilization; indeed, it must be confessed that even the hotels in the chief seaports, such as Cattaro, would seem rather rough to the sybarite. We met with universal kindness and civility, and even honesty, throughout Dalmatia, from the Austrian officers and officials, as well as from the Sclav and Italian population. We found every one anxious to go out of their way to point out to us the lions of the district. The tariff at the hotels is very low, as it is, by the way, on the Austrian Lloyds, where the two really excellent meals provided daily at one and eight, cost one and one-and-a-half florins (paper) respectively. In short, one lives luxuriously for about five shillings a day. The officers are gentlemanly and well-educated men—Dalmatians or Italians, as a rule—and very glad to fraternize with jovially-disposed English passengers. One is almost sure to find one or more who speak English. We took our tickets for Spalato, at which very interesting town we determined to stay for a few days. This is but a two-hundred miles' run from Trieste, but forty-two hours are spent in the passage. For though very little merchandize is taken on board at the several ports touched at, in order to pick up mails and passengers, a most unnecessary amount of time is wasted in each. Of this of course we are not sorry. Now the steamer would anchor off some picturesque little town, such as Pirano, crowned by its ancient fortress—a relic of the great republic which once ruled all this coast—and now bring up alongside the marble quay of some ancient Roman city, such as Pola, with its gigantic amphitheatre reflected on the purple Adriatic.

The scenery of the coast is very beautiful. The mountains are lofty and fantastically serrated, and cleft into profound fissures and chasms; while innumerable islands surround one on every side, so that one seems to be sailing on a large lake rather than a sea. Each turn round some jagged promontory reveals some new wonder, and there is not a village that is not picturesque and antique, with Venetian fortress or Byzantine church rising from the very water's edge. It is impossible to say what colour the Adriatic is; it is certainly the most chameleon-like of seas, and changes its hue quite irrespectively, as far as I could see, of atmospheric influence, under a sunny sky from deepest violet to most delicate turquoise, but ever beautiful.

However, after a time, there is something remarkably wearisome in this coast; for though the mountains are grandly formed, they are almost universally barren, the vegetation being scant and trees exceedingly rare. The Venetians made the most of their possessions when they had them, and destroyed the once magnificent forests of Illyria in a most ruthless manner. Nearly all the timber for their fleets was procured from these mountains.

The result is, that they are hopelessly bleak and barren, while the country in many places presents for miles inland the appearance of a stony desert. I do not think there is a region in Europe so wild and desolate as the plains in the neighbourhood of Novegrad; however, I believe that further inland, and so almost inaccessible, large and fine forests abound.

The weather was mild enough now, in the latter end of September (80° Fahr. in the shade), but this is a frightfully hot and parched-up country in the summer. The vegetation, where there is any, is sub-tropical; the date-palm, the aloe, and the cactus, are seen springing here and there from the rocks; citrons, pomegranates, almonds, are cultivated in many parts of the Lowlands.

We steamed slowly on throughout the day, till the setting sun lit up the high Dinaric Alps, which is a precipitous and unbroken line, lowered in the background above the lesser maritime chains. The barren precipices assumed the most lovely tints, in some places glowing like molten iron, while the shadows toned down to a deep hazy purple. But soon the sun had forsaken the loftiest peak, and the quick-coming darkness reminded us that our supper was spread in the comfortable cabin. The day had been a very enjoyable one, for the scenery and inhabitants were alike new to us. Our deck passengers were lying about in most picturesque groups. Here some Hungarian recruits devouring their rations greedily; here some wild-looking Dalmatian Morlaks; here a solemn Turkish merchant, puffing at his long pipe; Montenegrins, Greeks, and an ugly-looking lot of felons, manacled and chained together, completed the scene. We had touched at Pirano, Parenzo, and Rovigno, in the morning. As our vessel brought up alongside the quay at Pola, we were enabled to stretch our legs for an hour on shore. We might have had two hours had it not been for the extreme deliberation and prudence with which the officers of these steamers approach a quay.

The vociferations and evident anxiety of every one on board whenever this operation had to be performed would lead one to suppose that it required extraordinary delicacy and skill, and was attended with no small risk. Our captain was evidently excessively pleased and proud whenever he had safely accomplished this duty, and looked round with a very self-satisfied and admire-me-if-you-please air as he wiped the perspiration from his brow.

So deep was the water, and so unobstructed the harbour, that one would have imagined it would have been easy to have steamed the vessel right up to her berth, but that is not the way they do things here.

When we were about half-a-mile off the shore a boat was lowered, which took out at a cable to a large buoy in the roads; then it was found that the line attached to the cable was not long enough to reach the buoy, so we had to steam a little nearer. When, after a good deal of bungling, we succeeded in making fast our bow to this buoy, another cable was taken from our stern to the quay; and, while the first was being gradually slacked out, our donkey-engine slowly coiled up the second cable and drew the vessel stern foremost to her berth.

However, with all these precautions, we did not make fast without some accident. One of our passengers, an Austrian naval officer, who was contemplating the proceedings through his eyeglass, got in the way of a warp, when it tautened suddenly, caught him in the middle, and projected him into the sea. Great excitement ensued, but he was soon rescued by a soldier on the quay, who hooked him up with his bayonet.

We were accompanied on shore by a fellow-passenger whose acquaintance we had made, a smart-looking young Turkish officer of gendarmerie. He was an Albanian Christian, a native of Scutari, and had just returned from a journey to Trieste. As this was the first time he had left his native country, he was amazed and pleased at all he saw; but he had evidently formed no high idea as to the moral character of the Europeans. The amazing wickedness of the Triestines was a theme on which he harped throughout the journey.

Pola is the head-quarters of the Austrian navy; there were three or four of their finest vessels there at the time. We observed that the proportion of officers and men to the number of ships was very great. Our Turk came with us to visit the remains of the Roman amphitheatre, one of the finest in Europe. The Romans he had never heard of, but had been informed on good authority that the massive edifice before him had been constructed in one day by the devil. We all had supper together on board this evening, and had a most amusing conversation with our new friend over our coffee and subsequent pipe and grog. He could speak and write Turkish, French, Italian, Albanese, and Sclave.

We naturally wished to learn from him what sort of a country Albania was, whether travelling was comparatively safe, and how we ought to set to work.

"Albania is perfectly safe," he said; "safer than Trieste. There are no banditti; you can walk alone from Scutari to Salonika, and be treated as a friend by all, especially as you are an Englishman."

What our friend understood by "perfectly safe" was not exactly what a timid tourist would understand by the term. On being questioned as to the police system, he replied: "Well, it is not in an exceedingly happy condition just now, for having received no pay or rations for fourteen months, the gendarmes have struck work."

"And how do you get on without them?"

"Oh, just as well as with them; we Albanians do not require police; we understand what is just, and can take the law into our own hands; the police always were useless. In a wild country like ours, a criminal—a murderer, for instance—can always escape them; he takes refuge in the mountains, and the gendarmerie know better than to follow him there. If we trusted to them, there would be no security for life or property; but this is how we manage. If, for instance, a man murdered me and fled, my family are bound to revenge my death; if they cannot find the murderer himself, they kill one of his family."

"Does not this system lead to a good many lives being sacrificed over one quarrel?"

"It acts well as a rule. But, as you say, it does lead to some bloodshed. Just before I left Scutari a man shot another's pig, which had strayed into his field; the owner of the pig immediately walked over to the other man's house and blew his brains out, which he was bound to do as a man of honour; then a relation of the slain man shot a relation of the other behind his back as he strolled into the bazaar, totally unaware of the existence of any quarrel between the families."

"Was that looked upon as fair play?"

"Everything is fair in our blood feuds. This very man was himself shot a few days afterwards as he was coming out of a mosque, by the brother of the man he had killed, who was waiting for him behind a wall. Several others on both sides were killed in this pig dispute, till at last the two families met and settled the matter amicably, and without dishonour to either party, for it was shown that an equal amount of damage had been inflicted on both families—ten men of one having been slain; nine men, one woman, and a pig of the other."

Our friend told us that he himself had a blood

feud on hand, and had to keep a very sharp look out.

I noticed that his hand was bandaged, and inquired how he had hurt it.

"Oh," he said, "I scratched it with my sabre, and so poisoned it. I have enemies at Scutari, and some months ago expected to be murdered any day; but, determining to kill some of them first, when the time came poisoned my sabre with a strong animal poison. I accidentally scratched myself with it one day. Luckily the poison was nearly rubbed off by that time, but as it was it very nearly took me out of this world."

Many other little anecdotes we extracted from our friend, all illustrative of the extreme security of Albania. Among other things we were warned never to allow people to walk close behind us; not to pay excessive attention to the lady portion of the population—that being the most frightful crime that one can be guilty of in that country.

We played at dominoes, drank grog, and discoursed on various topics till a late hour; then retired for the night, during which the old vessel steadily steamed her eight knots an hour.

The Austrian Lloyd Company are bound, by their contract with the Government, not to run their vessels at a higher speed; why, no one could inform us.

On awakening the next morning we found ourselves moored to the quay of the fine old town of Zara. We went on shore with our new friend, who, by the way, was saluted by the Austrian officers and soldiers when they observed his uniform—an honour which we afterwards found was rarely paid him by his own men in Scutari, in the present discontented condition of the half-starved Turkish soldiery. We had time to visit the monuments of this interesting old Venetian fortress, the fine churches, and the magnificent cathedral, built by Doge Dandolo.

The streets are narrow, sewerless, and malodorous; but would be the delight of artists. The natives wear a particularly picturesque costume, but are exceedingly dirty, and not prepossessing in features.

I had somehow or another formed an idea that as we advanced southwards into the more uncivilized countries of Herzegovina, Montenegro, and Albania, we should find that the population, as it became more and more artistic in appearance, would at the same time become more and more dirty and villanous-looking. Seeing how very nasty these Dalmatians were, I expected to come across something very horrible indeed later on. In this I must say that I was agreeably disappointed; for all these reputedly barbarous races are far more intelligent, clean, and handsome, than the dull and in every way objectionable Morlak of Southern Austria, who much resembles his brother the Bulgarian.

One of the natives of this district writes thus of his countrymen:—

"For every article of necessity and comfort Dalmatia is dependent on other countries. There is clay, but no potter; quartz, but no glass-work; timber, but no carpenter; lime, but no kiln; coal, but no mine; iron, but no furnace; rags (plenty of them), but no paper-mill."

These words, written some years ago, are almost true of the present day. The wretched condition of the country is partly due to the régime of the Venetians, who got what they could out of it, but did little for the improvement of the people. The greater portion of the territory was acquired by Austria from Venice in 1798.

But though the Government has established schools, and a university at Zara, and done much in many ways to ameliorate the condition of things, Dalmatia is still in a very backward condition. The natives look with suspicion on, and are far from grateful for, the benefits they receive from the State. The Austrians are cordially hated by both the Sclavs and the Italians. These two latter, again, are very jealous of each other. So great is the mutual dislike, that it is rare to find even two fellow-townsmen of the different races on anything like friendly terms.

To a casual observer, at any rate, it seems that Austria has no very secure footing in this country, and has effected a mere military occupation of it.

The Government does its best to conciliate the people. They are lightly taxed, and have been allowed to retain many important rights and privileges.

The population has been disarmed by the Austrians, who are now carrying out the same policy in the Herzegovina and Bosnia — their lately acquired possessions.

Thus the Morlaks—who, like their neighbours in the Turkish provinces, were wont to stalk about bristling with pistols and knives, even in the towns—are now obliged to be contented with enormous red ginghams, which have become quite a feature in the national costume.

Luckily for Austria, three-quarters of the population are Roman Catholics, those of the Greek Church being the minority; thus Russian intrigue, though it is carried on by numerous agents, does not effect much harm among the Sclavs of these districts.

After having visited the many objects of interest in this old Venetian city, and having tried and highly approved of the Rosoglio and Maraschino, for the manufacture of which it is now celebrated, we returned to our vessel, and were soon once more steaming down the ever-changing coast to the southwards.

The sky was obscured by clouds and the wind was strong; but there was little sea, for the islands were so frequent that we but rarely caught a glimpse of the open Adriatic. The shores, both of continent and island, were very stony and barren. There seemed to be no cultivation or any sign of life for miles. I should say that there must be thousands of uninhabited islands along this coast.

We had for some time been silently smoking our cigarettes on the bridge, observing the desolate panorama as it swept by us, when our Turk suddenly broke in with—

"Why do not you English, who are so strong, and take a part so often in other people's quarrels, fight for yourselves and recover what Buonaparte took from you."

I was obliged to confess that I did not quite understand to what he was alluding.

"Ah, your countrymen never confess to a defeat. But tell me, is not England a triangle in shape?"

"It is true."

"So I have been told. Now how long is it since she has been of that form?"

Not being able to give any reply to this difficult query, he enlightened my ignorance.

"I have been told that when Buonaparte made an alliance with the Russians and the Italians, he beat England, and each of the three powers took from her a slice — thus leaving her triangular in shape. Is it not so?"

While he spoke he drew an imaginary diagram in the air with his sabre, illustrative of this unfortunate episode in our history. Our friend was utterly unaware that England was surrounded by the seas. His idea was that our empire consisted of an extensive region bordering on Russia, of which India was a province.

He was very anxious to learn if there were Sclavs in England; whether Queen Victoria was a Sclav; whether the English did not assume a blackish-brown complexion in the winter, in consequence of the perpetual fog. I tried to enlighten him on some of these matters, but I do not think he placed any credence in a word I said, though he was too polite to exhibit his incredulity.

With the assistance of the donkey-engine we brought up alongside the quay of Sebenico, and there remained for about half-an-hour. I find in my diary this one note: "Sebenico does not smell nice." This was a first impression.

On my return journey I visited this town, and well worthy of a visit it is.

It is built on the slope of a steep mountain, and

rises from the water's edge in an amphitheatre of quaint old buildings, a colossal Venetian fortress dominating all. The approach to it from the sea is remarkable. A labyrinth of narrow channels between rocky islands affords a difficult access to the shipping.

The Canale de St. Antonio—the one by which the steamer enters the port—is in one place so shut in by the precipitous islands, that it seems as if one could touch either side of it from the deck with outstretched arm. The streets are narrow, dirty, and steep; but some of the houses are very lofty and quaint, and all are impressed with the solemn and grandiose character of the Venetian style.

We steamed on through the afternoon, which was wild and stormy. The setting sun lit up the lofty and gloomy mountains of the Herzegovina, which far away inland towered above the lesser intervening heights, with a lurid light, while fierce gusts, driving black clouds before them, swept down the ravines till they struck our vessel in violent squalls which heeled her over, and sent the white spray hissing over the small rocky islands which jutted out everywhere to leeward of us.

At nine o'clock this evening we were alongside the quay of Spalato. Bidding adieu to our friends on board, and promising our Turk to visit him at Scutari, we threw our baggage into

SPALATO.

a small boat manned by some ragged and noisy ruffians, whose language was so rapid and so horrible in sound, that I could not but admire them for their evident ability to understand each other, and inwardly formed a higher opinion of the intellectual capacity of this branch of the Sclav race at any rate.

CHAPTER III.

Dalmatian *cuisine*—The Emperor Diocletian—Remains of the old palace—We make two friends—Wines of Dalmatia—Customs of the Morlaks—A visit to Salona—A great fête—Costumes—Morlak singing.

ON landing we were at once pounced upon by the Custom-house officers, who could not quite make out our semi-military appearance. Our baggage, however, was not examined, so our cartridges once more escaped. Re-shouldering our guns, and handing over our blankets and saddle-bags to a quay-loafer, we marched off to the Hôtel de Ville, which we were told is the best inn in the town. A very fair one it turned out to be, consisting of the first and second floor of a portion of a large desolate-looking collonaded square, recently built by a company, whose shareholders I believe will willingly part with their shares at the price of issue, for they have not met with much encouragement to continuing their work. The telegraph and post-offices, and the restaurant of the hotel, at present monopolize the completed portion of the square. On the other unbuilt side is a sulphur spring, not sufficiently appreciated by the faculty of Spalato.

The restaurant adjoining the hotel is a fair one for this country, but the cuisine of Dalmatia can hardly be recommended. The dishes presented to the traveller are not exactly German, nor are they exactly Italian, but combine the worst properties of the two without any of the good. On the other hand, the rooms in this hotel are very clean and comfortable, and the charge at this, as at all other restaurants on this coast, is considerably lower than in most countries of Europe. Having dined, we strolled through the town, whose nightly aspect we did not think very much of.

Instinct led us to the principal café. It is in the piazza in the centre of the town, and is greatly frequented by the Austrian officers as well as by the local civil swells. The open-air part of the café is a pleasant arbour of sub-tropical creepers. Here we smoked our cigarettes, and sipped our iced coffee for an hour or so, amused with the quaint costumes of the people and the lofty houses around us, dating from the old Venetian days, as their elegant porticoes and fine carvings plainly showed. On the wall of one house near the café there are some very curious religious carvings. Eve presenting the apple to Adam is very comic.

Spalato is a town at which one could easily pass a considerable time in most enjoyable loafing. The old Venetian city is built within the extensive walls of the palace of Diocletian, but the modern town has spread considerably beyond their limits. These ancient walls formed a useful defence against the piratical hordes that infested this coast during the Middle Ages, till the strong arm of the Venetian Republic swept the Adriatic of these freebooters, whose detestable excesses were the terror of the whole maritime population.

Spalato is built on a promontory formed by the deep inlet on whose shores is situate the old Roman city of Salona, while the large islands of Brazza and Bua shelter the harbour from on-shore winds.

It was to this pleasant spot that the Emperor Diocletian, himself a native of Salona, retired in the year 305, when, weary of empire, he resigned the imperial purple. On the sea-shore, a few miles from Salona, he built himself this magnificent palace, in which he passed the remainder of his life without care or regret, taking great pleasure in cultivating his garden with his own hands.

The outer walls form a square, each side of which is nearly a mile in length. These to a great measure still exist, but the modern houses built against and *into* them have by no means improved their appearance. The Cathedral of

Spalato was the Pagan Temple which Diocletian constructed in the centre of the area, and is a very symmetrical building. Many of the columns, and also the Sphinx, which ornament the palace, were brought here from Constantinople and Egypt.

We were awakened early the next morning by a knock at our door. On our replying to it a pleasant-looking stout gentleman entered smiling, and introduced himself to us as Marco Bettoni, *capitaine de long cours*. He had heard of the arrival of two Englishmen in the town, so as he spoke English himself, he had come to offer his services to us. A very useful and agreeable companion he proved to be. The Dalmatians are excellent sailors, and these retired *capitaines de long cours* form a most respectable element in the population. Most of the *Podestas* or mayors of the small villages are of this class. They are always men who have knocked about the world, and are happy to assist travellers in every way.

After breakfast we visited some of the lions of Spalato, in the company of our new friend. The architecture of the narrow streets, with their lofty balconied houses, and the ever-recurring Lion of St. Mark carved over the archways, constantly reminded one of the old Republic. We went to the "Porta Aurea"—the "golden gate," which pierces the outer wall of Diocletian's palace from the north. I sat down under a blazing sun, and managed to make a sketch of it. During the process I was surrounded by a crowd of admiring Morlaks. When the marble columns which supported the arches were in their places, it must have been very beautiful. The ancient Temple of Jupiter, now the Cathedral of Spalato, was within the precincts of the palace. It is now surmounted by an elegant *campanile*, which was constructed after its conversion into a Christian church. From the summit of this—200 feet above the sea—there is a charming view over the town, the harbour, and the islands of the Adriatic beyond.

The interesting remains of this town have been so well described by former travellers, that I will not here enter into them. Suffice to say that Spalato offers at every step some curious relic of early Christian as well as Pagan days, not to mention the fine Venetian buildings. In the architecture of the palace as well as in the statuary brought from Salona, and stored here in the public museum, one can detect the transition state of art, and the falling off of the old classic beauty of form.

We were introduced by our new friend to a very pleasant French gentleman, who was of great service to us during our stay. M. Vigneau was an *Ænologue*, a native of Bordeaux, and had come hither to be manager of a company recently started at Spalato, for the production of superior classes of wines. The natives of the country were quite ignorant of the science, their wines being rough and unpalatable—surcharged with tannin. But, under the scientific and skilful direction of M. Vigneau, it has been proved that Dalmatia is capable of producing excellent wines, emulating the finest vintages of his native land. Other companies have since his attempt been started for the like purpose, but as far as I could judge the "*Société Œnologue de Dalmatie,*" as the orignal Spalato undertaking is called, produces the largest variety and most excellent quality of wines.

We visited the buildings of the company. It was the vintage season, and huge butts were brimming with the ripe fruit outside the door. In the yard two employés sat at a table purchasing the grapes, as picturesque Morlaks—men, women, and children—bore in the purple spoil in sacks and baskets of every size. These were weighed, and the little bundles of money were handed over to them in return. Now and then a basket would be refused, the quality of grape being inferior; when the wild people would enter into a fierce discussion with many gesticulations, but were peremptorily told to move on, as their noise was useless. The Mórlaks are civilized enough to know some of the tricks of trade spoken of by the "divine Artemus" as common among the American manufacturers of apple-sauce, the difference being that in the one case the bottom of the vessel is filled with sawdust and in the other with stones.

We indulged in a feast of grapes at M. Vigneau's, and then adjourned to his spacious cellars to try his various wines. The huge casks, which contain enough of the rich fluid to drown the largest elephant, had been brought in sections from Bordeaux—the natives being incapable of constructing them. The wines we tasted were exceedingly good, and the different varieties might pass for the best burgundies, sherries, and ports; there is also an excellent light wine. These wines are improved by a sea voyage. They are cheap, and need only to be introduced into England to be appreciated and widely consumed. Indeed I am sure many of us have unknowingly drunk and enjoyed them, for M. Vigneau told me that not only were large quantities exported to Italy, but—especially since the Phylloxera plague had broken out—also to France, to the Bordeaux district itself, where doubtlessly they are blended with the native product and sent to us under many fair-sounding Châteaux brands.

The Sclav names which the Spalato wines bear are not musical. M. Vigneau gave me all the details and prices. These wines could be sold in

England, after paying all transport and custom expenses, at a very low rate indeed. The company is sufficiently old for us to have tasted and approved some choice vintages that had been twelve years or so in bottle, and very excellent they proved.

M. Vigneau had spent a few years in England, and speaks English very well. So between him and the kindly old sea-captain, we did not feel ourselves at all abroad in Spalato. Without them we should not have got on, for our knowledge of Italian was limited, and of Sclav we knew but the names for bare necessaries. At Spalato we had many opportunities of observing the manners and customs of the mixed population of the Dalmatian coasts.

The native Italians and Sclavs keep very much to themselves. There is no society of any kind, and I cannot say I was in any way favourably impressed with them. The Austrian garrison, officers and men, on the other hand, created a very favourable impression. There is none of that swagger and bounce which is too often displayed by the troops of some nations we know of when in the midst of a subject alien and hostile race. The officers are very gentlemanly-looking men, and the Hungarians who were quartered here struck one by their jovial and kindly manners.

The Austrian officers much dislike service in this province; it is the Siberia of Austria. The people do not speak their tongue, and will not mix with them; and the upper classes studiously insult them, as far as they dare. The Morlaks or Sclav peasantry are an interesting race, but not much to be admired.

They are from all accounts great thieves and liars, and more backward, I should say, than any people in Europe. They have no desire for improvement. Any one who endeavours to introduce some new manufacture or industry among them is treated with suspicion; every obstacle is studiously thrown in his way.

The costumes of the male Morlaks are very picturesque, varying in different districts. They wear the baggy trousers coming to the knee; the embroidered vest and red sash of the East. In most parts the head-dress is a skull-cap, flat at the top, sometimes red; generally the colour is indistinguishable for the accumulated grease of years. They wear *opunkas* on their feet. These are sandals or slippers, with turned-up toe; made of rough thongs of oxhide; they are tied to the foot with straps of the same material. The Morlak is always accompanied by his long pipe with its red clay bowl. He is also addicted to smoking cigarettes through brightly painted wooden tubes fully three feet in length. The dress of the women differs so much in districts that it is impossible to give anything like a general description of it; it is not unlike that of the Southern Italians. They, too, wear the opunka.

The Morlaks have many strange superstitions and customs. To any one who wishes to see in the life the barbarous manners of the Middle Ages in all their picturesqueness, a voyage in these countries can be recommended. However, the Austrians have eliminated one of the most picturesque, if rather objectionable, features of the good old times. Hordes of brigands no longer overrun Dalmatia; the vendetta is now unknown; and travelling, if rough, is unattended with danger; and I may add that Morlaks, despite their other faults, are exceedingly hospitable, and will give up their one bed to the travelling stranger.

The women of this race are treated in true Eastern fashion; that is, not much better than the beasts of burden.

As in the East, those of the higher class rarely leave their houses, but sit lazily in their chamber acquiring a becoming pallor of countenance and fatness of limb. A Sclav will not allude to his wife in conversation without an apology for mentioning so low a thing. "My wife, excuse me, sir," is the common way of bringing her into a sentence. As in the East, too, the unchaste woman is regarded with great abhorrence. What vice there may be has to conceal itself in dark places, for the old punishment of the stoning is by no means unknown here. In the towns of Albania, this outward show of morality—for that is all it really is, just as in the old days, when the virtuous man to throw the first stone was not to be found—is still more ferociously demonstrative, cases of guilty parties of both sexes having been torn to pieces by the mob being of not unfrequent occurrence there.

The following incident happened shortly before our arrival at Scutari. A Turkish officer of police, who had carried on a flirtation with the German servant of a foreign consul, was discovered, seized by several men, and beaten till he fainted with his wounds, and was left by them for dead.

The next day was Sunday. Hiring a trap, we drove, with our two friends, along a good road, across a wine-producing country, commanding pleasant views of sea and mountain, to Salona— the old Roman city—the birthplace of Diocletian. It is but four miles from Spalato. As we approached it we saw, some miles off inland, on a precipitous buttress of the mountain, the ancient and impregnable fortress of Clissa, commanding the approach to Spalato from the Herzegovina.

Salona is situated on the sloping ground at the head of the deep and beautiful inlet of the sea, which bears the same name. The ruins have been excavated, and there are no important remains to be seen, for the town was thoroughly sacked and destroyed by the Gothic hordes. It was from Salona, in 544, that Belisarius set out to rescue Italy from Totila and his Goths. The town had withstood several sieges. Attila himself is reported to have once captured it. Having for years enjoyed peace, lulled into a false and fatal sense of security, the Salonites, the historian tells us, gradually fell into a state of incredible luxury and sensuality. This was the Sybaris of the East. At last the day of trial came, and the effete citizens were found to be incapable of defending their homes against the hardier foe.

The Avars overrun Dalmatia in the year 639.

Salona easily fell into the hands of the Barbarians. The sinful city was plundered and burnt to the ground; and where stood its stately theatres and temples, there is now but an uninhabited wilderness.

Its site commands a splendid view over the blue gulf, and dark, far mountains. This day, at this season of the year, when a brown tint was on the tangled groves, and a purple bloom on the grapes, while a fresh sea wind sighed through the desolate ruins, the general effect was very impressive.

Here we wandered a couple of hours or so through vines and brushwood, the fallen walls of houses, tombs, shattered friezes and columns meeting us at every turn. Nearly everywhere, on raking off the thin layer of overlying rubbish, beautiful tessalated pavements are disclosed to view. The Morlak peasantry crowded round us and sold to us, at ridiculously low prices, coins of the Diocletian era, vases and beautiful lacrymals, irridescent and scaling off with age. Several were melted out of shape by the fires of that fierce sacking more than a thousand years ago.

The Roman aqueduct which supplied the palace of Diocletian, at Spalato, with water, is still in very fair repair.

The modern city suffers much from want of water. This necessary has to be carted in from a long distance.

The restoration of the old aqueduct has been decided on; and to have come to a decision will suffice the Dalmatians for some years to come. It is to be hoped that the plan will ultimately be carried out. "The Spalatans will then have no excuse left for not washing themselves;" so I said to Mr. Vigneau, innocently. " Oh, you don't know them," said he; " they will discover that washing opens the pores, and renders them more susceptible to the *trebesine* (the fever)."

The source of the *Gindro*, where commences the aqueduct, is well worthy of a visit. About a mile from Salona—at the head of a wild and beautiful well-wooded gorge down which this torrent flows—the further progress of the traveller is barred by a precipitous wall of rock. At the foot of this wall an enormous volume of ice-cold water rushes out upwards from an orifice in the rock, filling up a deep, broad pool, which foams and whirls as the spring spouts up from underneath with incredible force, forming a dome of water on the surface. There is something horrible in the Titanic forces and furious whirl, that makes one dizzy; one cannot look down long. The water overflowing from the pool partly feeds the aqueduct, which is carried along the slope of the hill, and partly rushes down the gorge, turning on its way the huge wheel of a flour-mill.

This mill we visited with M. Vigneau. The enterprising individual who had started it seemed very disheartened. The latest machinery had been brought hither at great cost. But this was too great a novelty for the conservative Morlak peasantry, who resented and fought shy of the innovation, preferring to grind their corn between two flat stones picked up in the river bed, as their fathers did before them.

We drove home before sunset, as there was much fever about. There was not a cottage near here that had not some of its occupants prostrated by the *trebesine*.

Tuesday, September the 30th, was a great Dalmatian holiday. On foot, on mule-back, in the rough waggons drawn by diminutive oxen, the peasantry trooped in. The Morlaks are very fond of feasts. Every other day seems to be dedicated to some saint or other, who would avenge himself were he neglected. The working days are few, as M. Vigneau bitterly complained.

I believe this peasantry still observes several feasts whose origin dates back to Pagan times.

The holiday gave us a good opportunity of viewing the various costumes of this country at their best.

Not least quaint were the Jews of Spalato. Some were long-bearded, solemn-looking old fellows, dressed in the same sombre garb the Jews of Venice wore when Shylock drove sharp bargains on the Rialto.

The groups that filled the narrow streets were very Eastern in appearance. The pig-tailed Morlak, clad in his Sunday jacket; the savage-looking Bosnian Turk, with turban, broad sash, and gay slippers; the Greek sailors; all had an outlandish appearance, that told us we were far from home—" from home and beauty" too, for of the latter there was little to be seen at Spalato. I honestly saw no women who could, with the grossest flattery, be called pretty, between Trieste and Montenegro. And what can make one feel so alone in a strange land, as the absence of fair women.

The Dalmatian Sclavs are unfortunately very

fond of raising their voices in song. A gang of youths would walk down a street arm-in-arm, shouting some native ballad. The music and singing of the East is always of a melancholy character; but never have I heard anything so dismal as the barbaric dirges of the Morlaks. The song is a sort of monotonous chant, which has a peculiar querulous complaining spirit in it; and yet a suppressed and timorous complaining, as of slaves that had not for centuries known what independence and freedom was.

How different is the song of the free Montenegrin (of the same race as the Morlak). It is of the same monotonous character, but has a go and energy in it, inspired as it is with the warlike feats of their heroes in the present as well as in the past —not a song of regret for some by-gone greatness, but an exultation in the brave and illustrious now.

Each verse of a Morlak song dies away in a long and sad howl, followed by a silence, before the next verse is taken up. This produces a peculiarly depressing effect.

Our arrival was pretty well known all over the town, for strangers are not frequent, especially Englishmen. The citizens, who could not conceive any one being mad enough to travel for amusement, especially in their country, discussed us curiously. M. Vigneau told us he had, several times each day, to give a long narrative of the lives, pursuits, &c., of Brown and myself, in order to satisfy the eager inquirers.

On hearing that we intended to visit Albania, the verdict always was, "They will not come back"—this with a meaning shrug of the shoulders.

I have, on more than one occasion found, when I have left England for some unknown and supposed dangerous country, that as I gradually neared it the reports and accounts of the perils of that land became less and less alarming. For "distance" lends terror as well as enchantment "to the view."

In the case of Albania, however, the nearer we approached it the worse was the reputation of its fierce inhabitants for murder and robbery; the more earnestly were we warned against travelling in such a cut-throat region. This was not an encouraging sign. However, the best plan is ever to go on as far as one can, and believe little one hears.

CHAPTER IV.

Voyage to Cattaro—A Bora—The gulf of Narenta—The Herzegovina — The island of Curzola — Ragusa — The Bocche di Cattaro—The frontier of Montenegro—The fortress of Cattaro—Evening promenade—Personal attractions of the Cattarine ladies—Rough roads—Prince Nikita's coach—Bosnian refugees—A Bosnian's luggage.

We had been in Spalato nearly a week. The steamers from Trieste did not bring us Jones and Robinson, so we determined to push on. We bid adieu to our good friends, who evidently considered our heads doomed to fall beneath Albanian yataghans, and embarked on October the 2nd at 4 p.m., on an Austrian Lloyd, bound for Cattaro, which lies up a long gulf at the foot of the Montenegrin mountains. There we were to leave civilization and the sea coast, and commence our inland march. From Spalato to Cattaro is a forty-eight hours' journey by the steamer. For the last few days the genial Scirocco, or south-east wind, had been blowing; but to-day the fierce gusts of the Bora, or north-east wind, had changed, in a trice, the warm autumn weather to bitter winter.

. This wind beats very heavily on the eastern coast of the Adriatic, and is much dreaded by seamen.

The quaint lateen craft of the country, constructed on such antique lines, skimmed by us with close-reefed sails—curious sails they are, many-coloured, and painted with pictures of suns and grotesque saints. Throughout the wild afternoon and night we steamed on, touching at Almissa and Macarsca on our way. The next day we steamed up the long, land-locked gulf of Narenta. The scenery, as usual, was fine, but so indescribably desolate and barren that the eye soon wearied of it. On the gulf of Narenta a narrow strip of Herzegovina runs down to the sea, thus, till that province was acquired by Austria, dividing her territory in two.

We anchored off a spot called Neoum, which is on this recently acquired slip, in order to land soldiers and munitions for the troops. Neoum is a military post recently established by Austria on the bare sides of the mountain. We landed, and found a barrack, a telegraph station, and a public-house; these were the only buildings. It is an important position, however, as being the nearest point to Mostar, in Herzegovina, to which town the Government is now constructing a military road from here. Next we touched at the picturesque fortress of Curzola, on the island of the same name. It is surrounded by grand old Venetian walls and towers, which rise from the water's edge.

This night we anchored for several hours off Gravosa, the northern harbour of Ragusa. The latter wonderful old city, perhaps the most interesting of all Dalmatia, we had time to explore in a rapid way.

There was once a Republic of Ragusa. The fact that it successfully maintained its independence, when all the surrounding countries had been acquired by Venice, will testify to the strength of the little state. The chief street is broad, and contains lofty and noble houses—residences of the old merchant princes—strong-built, with elegant balconies and carved porticoes. From this street narrow streets ascend the mountain side, in steps of granite. Arches are thrown from house-top to house-top; there are some grand bits for a painter. The town is paved with broad, flat stones, which gives it a very clean appearance.

The next was a glorious day. The gentle south wind once more brought summer back to us, and the lateen-rigged boats again shook out their reefs, and displayed all their gaudy canvas.

It was early in the day when we steamed through the entrance of the Bocche di Cattaro.

This magnificent fiord has often been described. It certainly contains some of the finest scenery in Europe.

The deep gulf winds into the heart of the wild Montenegrin mountains. At first it is quite six miles in width, then it narrows to a few hundred yards, then again widens into an extensive lake as the fantastically-shaped, almost perpendicular masses of bleak rock jut far out into the deep clear water in rugged promontories, or retire from it in dark and profound chasms and ravines.

Here and there houses and churches are seen perched on seemingly inaccessible ledges, thousands of feet above the blue water which reflects them. There are several small towns on the shores of the Bocche. Castelnuovo and Perasto have beautiful situations. Pleasant villages, half buried in olive gardens, are built on the lower slopes of the hills.

But the first view of that extraordinary fortress, Cattaro, is never to be forgotten. At the very head of the last arm of the Bocche the dark blue masses of mountain, here higher and more precipitous than elsewhere, shut in a deep bay.

More than 4000 feet above, on the ridge, is the frontier of Montenegro—a country by the sea,

BOCCHE DI CATTARO.

Page 48.

WALLS OF CATTARO.

looking down on the blue water, yet shut out from it by its big neighbours.

A bold bluff of rock, a thousand feet or more in height, slightly projects from the main mass, perpendicular, bare, cleft into profound chasms. This extraordinary site has been chosen for the most wonderful fortress in Europe. Below, on the narrow margin between rock and sea, is built the town. Along the water's edge is a quay, to which are moored the beautiful craft of the country. This has been converted into a pleasant walk, fringed with trees. Behind this is the old Venetian wall of the city, with its fine solid towers and broad battlements; the time-darkened stones in places luxuriantly overgrown with the lovely flowers and creepers of the sunny South. Passing through the portcullised gate, one enters into a strange, quaint city. The streets are narrow, the houses lofty, and covered with grotesque carvings. No carts, carriages, or horses, are permitted to enter the town. This, by-the-bye, is the case in most Dalmatian cities. The whole is paved with large flags. Cattaro is of some length, but very narrow, for it is shut in by the steep cliff which rises immediately from behind it.

Now the walls of the town, after bounding it on the sea front, zigzag up either side of the bluff I mentioned, till they meet on its crowning point, a thousand feet above the sea, where stands a formidable-looking castle.

On observing how they rise and dip, adapting themselves to the little ravines and irregularities of the rock, one is irresistibly reminded of the pictures of the great wall of China one was so much impressed with in the spelling-books of childhood.

Very old the town and fortifications are. No improving Goth has yet taken aught away from their grotesque grandeur.

It is very difficult to describe the effect of all this, for the scenery in and around Cattaro is such as is not to be found elsewhere, quite *sui generis*. The most *blasé* traveller would utter an exclamation of surprise when that wonderful fortress suddenly appeared before him, like some great city of the genii that one has read of in fairy tale, or seen in some half-remembered nightmare. The high cliff, with its grey fortress, seems ready to topple down on the town any moment. Some of the huge masses of overhanging rock have at times been dislodged, and fallen below; many of these are chained to the mountain, to prevent this catastrophe.

So lofty and steep are the surrounding heights that Cattaro does not enjoy much of the light of the sun; the shadows depart late, and soon set in. But during the few hours in the middle of the day that the sun's rays do fall on it, this place is like an oven—possibly the hottest town in Europe.

About four o'clock in the afternoon our steamer was alongside the quay. We marched off to the Hotel Cacciatore, a very decent place, whose proprietor is a quaint fellow, with a perpetual smile, who imagines he can speak French. The restaurant is fair, and frequented by the officers of the garrison. The custom-house officers did not trouble us, but the mosquitoes did; so, too, did certain insects that inhabited our beds.

Brown is one of those unfortunate people whose blood is exceptionally sweet and palatable to insect life, and to whom, consequently, the hours of darkness in these lands bring no peace, but sleepless torments worse than the guiltiest, liveliest conscience could inflict. He brought with him from England a large packet of insecticide, and every night, before he retired, made careful preparations to withstand the usual siege. He was not contented with dusting himself all over so freely that he set the whole Albanian expedition sneezing for an hour, but he would also build around his body, on the bed-clothes, an impregnable rampart of the powder so broad and lofty that the most active flea would fail to leap it.

The next day was Sunday—a warm and delicious day. We attended the service, and enjoyed the fine music in the old Venetian church. In the evening we visited the public promenade on the quay outside the walls, which was crowded by the population and the country people in their Sunday best.

At the end of this promenade there is a public garden, and a *café* under the ramparts. The marble tables are placed out of doors, among the bright flowers and creepers. Here we sat lazily smoking our cigarettes, and listening to the music of the Hungarian military band that played just in front of us. There is no gas at Cattaro; the town is lit with petroleum. The band carries its own lamps. It was curious to see the men troop into the garden, each with a pole over his shoulder, to which hung his lit lantern. This place is really delightful on such an evening as this. The scene was exactly like some great scenic display on the boards of a large theatre—some dream of fairyland. One could not help half expecting to see some bright Eastern ballet trip in the next moment. The promenade in front of the walls was the stage and proscenium. The lovely Eastern night, the moon hanging over the great hills, the blue waters and the fantastic shipping, the giant walls and towers, the grand mountains behind all, the picturesque crowd, and the lively music, all combined to form a perfect spectacle, magic-like—to say theatrical would be an unworthy adjective—that I, for my part, never imagined could be found within a week's journey of practical, ugly London, dear old place though it is.

Costumes flitted by us as brilliant and strange to the eye as those of an Alhambra *opera bouffe*. The Morlak, the lithe and bright-eyed Greek, the turbaned Turk of Bosnia, with glowing robe, solemn and haughtily-looking; the Montenegrin mountaineer, with his white coat tied on with silken sash, and richly embroidered vest; the Albanian in fez, snowy kilt, rough capote, and jacket stiff with gold; the Arnaut, with his manly tight-fitting dress, stalking through the crowd, looking the fierce and undaunted savage that he is—all these strolled or stood in groups, completing the picture with their richly-coloured and varied costume. The very Europeans, with their sadder-hued dress, formed no unpleasing foil to these.

The ladies, with unbonnetted heads, over which a shawl is gracefully thrown in Venetian fashion, their little feet silk-stocked and slippered, as in the East, above which, just peeping below the black silk dress, hung a mere suspicion of delicate white embroidered petticoat, were charming—if not seen too near: an ungallant verdict, reluctantly wrung from a veracious traveller.

The Hungarian and other Austrian uniforms were also no unpleasing feature in the throng.

I have just now, and I think on other occasions, used the term European in contradistinction to the term Dalmatian. I only follow the usage of the country. I found that Dalmatians and Albanians always spoke of Europe as if they were quite apart from it. "You Europeans," "you in Europe," was a common phrase.

The music ceases—the lights are extinguished. We must pass through the walls by the narrow gate into the city. By night the portcullis is half lowered, so we have to stoop to go through, as if to bow in obeisance to the winged lion of St. Mark that is carved in the old stone above.

We walked through the quaint old streets, whose broad clean flags rang metallically under our feet. The town was now deserted and silent. As we approached the hotel we stood and listened to one remarkable noise which can be heard once every hour at Cattaro, and which produces a very curious and pleasing effect. This is the watchword of the sentries on the walls. First, the sentinel below at the gate-tower commences, with the long wailing cry; then the next takes it up, then the next, and so on, right up the zigzag fortifications to the fortress up in the mountain, a thousand feet above, each cry fainter than the last. Then, when the sentinel at the extreme summit has shouted out the word—his voice almost inaudible to us so far below—it is carried down the other side of the walls, distincter and distincter again, until it reaches the starting-point again, and the man posted on the grim old tower just before us gives out in loud voice the last intimation that all is well.

We loafed about the neighbouring mountains and shores for some days, waiting to see if those dilatory travellers, Jones and Robinson, would turn up. We visited the new road now being constructed into Montenegro—a difficult undertaking to surmount these frightful rocks. The old road, which is carried in long zigzags from above Cattaro to the summit of the pass, is calculated to test the wind and muscles of the pedestrian. It is a very rough affair; and though much labour has been expended to clear away the larger rocks that obstruct the way, yet in some places one has to clamber over boulders of considerable height. The Montenegrins look upon this rough track as being a model high-road. It is far better than most of the so-called roads of Montenegro and Albania. But in these countries it is generally difficult to make out what is intended for road, and what is not. The roughest mule-track of Switzerland is as good as a great highway here.

The Prince of Montenegro recently paid a visit

to the Emperor of Austria, at Vienna, where he was made very much of. When he was about to return to his native mountains, the Emperor was much puzzled to know what would be a fitting present to make to the semi-barbaric despot. At last he bethought him of a splendid state-carriage, on whose panels were painted the arms of the principality, and four fine horses.

The Prince was much gratified, and the costly gift was taken by steam to Cattaro. Here an unexpected difficulty arose. The carriage could not be taken to Cettinje, for there was nothing that by the greatest stretch of compliment could be called a carriage-road leading into the principality. So here, at Cattaro, in Austria, the coach has to remain until the new road be completed, which will not be for some time to come. Whether the coach was originally given in anticipation of the new road, or whether the new road is being constructed for the coach, I was not able to discover.

On the next day the Duke of Wittemburg arrived here by steamer, on his way to Cettinje. A deputation of gorgeously-clad Montenegrin notables, tall, handsome, and straight, armed to the teeth was on the quay to receive him. These contrasted favourably with the municipal authorities, who were there for the same object. A German or Italian in swallow-tail coat, black silk hat, and white kid gloves, in broad sunlight, is an uncomfortable and unpleasing object.

In the afternoon the guns from the fort above the town fired twice—the signal that the Trieste steamer was in sight. This time we made certain that our friends were on board.

So confident were we, that Brown and myself tossed up as to whether Jones or Robinson should be at the charge of a bottle of maraschino to be consumed by the quartette.

We were again disappointed. We went on board; they were stowed away in no part of the vessel. The deck presented a curious appearance; it was crowded with turbaned Bosnian refugees, who with their wives and families, had deserted their native land, intolerable to them since its occupation by the Austrian giaours. They were now on their way to the new lands promised to them by the Porte. This exodus is much more extensive than is generally imagined. These poor people bore their grief with true Oriental apathy. They had laid their mats on the decks, and were squatting on them smoking silently, holding no converse with the hated giaours around them. The veiled women crouched up close under the bulwarks in a shrinking manner, while the little nude children sprawled about anywhere. I need not add that all swarmed with vermin. They had their Penates with them, of course. Their luggage was rather scanty.

It was a curious sight to see them trooping out of the vessel, each man bearing his *impedimenta*—his mat, pipe, and coffee-pot; this was all. One family had a European portmanteau; this was opened at the Custom-house. Its contents proved to be—on one side potatoes, on the other a coffee-pot! The potatoes doubtlessly had been dug from the little enclosure round the homestead in the old country.

We decided to give up our friends, and start on the morrow for Cettinje, the capital of Montenegro, for we had wasted some time, and were anxious to commence our march into the wild interior, and see what lay beyond that barrier of cloud-capped rock before us.

We found a Montenegrin who owned a small wiry mountain horse. He agreed for a small sum to guide us, and carry our baggage to the capital.

Before leaving Cattaro we changed some English sovereigns into swanzickers. This is an old Austrian coin, out of circulation in the Empire, of the date of Maria Theresa, and as a rule bearing her effigy. This is the coin particularly affected by the Montenegrins, they always value anything in these elsewhere obsolete swanzickers.

The Turkish modern coinage is also accepted, but under protest. The silver Medjidie seems to have a different value in every Montenegrin village. Austrian modern money or paper they will have nothing to do with, as a rule. Of course gold of any kind is readily taken.

The value of the English sovereign and French napoleon is well known all over eastern Europe. I was surprised to find that the humblest mountaineer in Albania knew the exact change for these pieces. The only difficulty in changing them lies in the possibility of a village not being able to muster a sufficiency of the small coin as an equivalent.

Bank-notes are of course useless in these wild countries; but at Cattaro and Spalato, and other Dalmatian towns, there are money-changers who will change these with pleasure.

When we were at Cattaro the pound sterling was worth eleven florins, sixty centimes, or thirty-three-and-a-half swanzickers.

CHAPTER V.

March to Cettinje—The pass across the frontier—Montenegrin warriors—Cettinje—A land of stones—The Prince's Hotel—Frontier disputes—The commission—Montenegrin method of making war—A game of billiards—A Draconic law—A popular prince.

EARLY on the morning of October the 9th, we commenced our journey in earnest. We passed through the land-side gate of the town, where our Montenegrin guide with the horse was awaiting us. Just outside this gate is the Montenegrin Bazaar, as it is called. It consists merely of two rough sheds built for the use of the Black Mountaineers, who come down to sell their produce at Cattaro. Here, too, before they enter the town, they are obliged to leave their mules and arms.

The latter was found to be a very necessary regulation, as quarrels which ended in bloodshed used often to occur between the fierce highlanders and the Cattarines. The two peoples are never on the best of terms—the former being accused of many a midnight descent into the valleys, to pillage and carry off all they can lay hands on. But the present Prince of Montenegro has to a great extent reformed his savage subjects.

A small Morlak boy was deputed by the Montenegrin to lead the horse, and guide us to the capital of the land of stones.

He was the proud possessor of a lockless Turkish pistol, which he stuck jauntily in his sash, and of which he was evidently very proud, for he would stop every now and then to readjust the formidable weapon.

It is not a six hours' march from Cattaro to Cettinje.

Every few yards of progress up the zigzag path revealed some new view over the indescribably grand gulf below.

At last we were far above town and fortress. They lay at our feet like a map. The eye could follow all the windings of the Bocche; and so high were we above it, that we could look over three successive chains of lofty mountains. The blue water stretched in three long streaks between them; while far away, over the furthest range, the blue Adriatic lay peacefully under a cloudless sky. It was a scene of unparalleled vastness and magnificence.

The summit of the pass was 4500, the fortress that tops the walls 1000 feet above the sea, by our aneroid.

We had chosen a gala day for our entry into Montenegro—for following, us a mile or so behind, were the Duke of Wittemburg and a numerous *cortège* on horseback, on their way to Prince Nikita's palace.

We turned a rocky bluff, and a stone marked the frontier of the huge Empire and little Principality.

Here, drawn up on the left side of the rough track, two deep, were about eighty armed, splendid-looking Montenegrins, awaiting to serve as guard of honour to the duke as far as the capital.

They were magnificent men, giants—all considerably above six feet in height, and broad in proportion. Each wore the long snowy coat of Montenegro—tied in with a broad sash. Their vests were red, and richly embroidered with gold and silk. Heavy plates formed of silver buttons covered their chests, well calculated to offer good resistance to sabre cut or bayonet.

They wore the national head-dress, which deserves a special description.

It is a round flat-topped cap of red cloth; round its side, and just overlapping its upper surface, is stitched a black band. In a corner of the red circle thus left at the top is embroidered a semicircle, in gold thread, into which is also often worked the initial letters of Prince Nikita's name in Sclav characters. This cap has a symbolical meaning. When the old Servian kingdom was broken up, and the South-western Sclavs became subject to strange races, the wild mountain district of Montenegro alone preserved its independence; so its inhabitants draped their red caps with black, in mourning for their enslaved brethren. The corner of gold on the red cloth is meant to represent Montenegro—the one corner of liberty on the field of blood—the one free spot of the old Sclav kingdom.

The sashes of these highlanders were stuck full of yataghans and pistols. Some were the richly-worked pistols of Albania, some the long Austrian grasser revolvers. This is the favourite small arm of the Montenegrins, who invariably scrape off the bluing when they purchase one of these weapons, as they consider it looks dirty, and prefer the bare steel.

Their guns were the Austrian breech-loading rifles of the old pattern; very fair weapons, but not to be compared to the Martini-Henrys which are so common in Albania.

These fine men—their plaids blowing to and fro with the fresh highland breeze, drawn up here on the savage mountain side, while the strains of the military band at Cattaro rose up from the abyss beneath—looked very imposing.

At Neigoussa, a miserable little village, there is

a *Khan*. Here we halted, gave our horses a feed, and sitting on the stone bench outside, lunched off goat's milk, cheese, and sausage, while the wild people, all armed to the teeth, crowded round us, and respectfully asked to be allowed to inspect our arms. His arms are the only things a Montenegrin loves and takes an interest in. He spends half his time in cleaning and polishing them. Our guns and revolvers were always much admired, and their systems had to be carefully explained at every halt. My revolver was the new army weapon, with patent extractor. This was something entirely novel to them. How often in this country or in Albania would some chief, covetous of the *Pushka Inglisi*, bring out a handful of coin, and say eagerly, "*Coliko, gospodiné,*" or "*Sa pare, Zutni?*" (How much, sir?), as the case might be. Our little guide had mastered its system, and would borrow it and proudly dilate on its excellencies to the men we met on the way.

At this *Khan*—having a large and appreciative audience round him—he favoured it with a lengthy lecture, with detailed explanations, followed, as far as I could make out, by a biography of the two English travellers. Startling it must have been, too, judging from the admiring and awe-struck way in which the men turned and stared at us during the narrative.

Early in the afternoon we marched down the

CETTINJE.

high-street, or rather the solitary street, of the smallest capital in Europe.

Cettinje is but a village of sordid huts, above which rises, imposing in contrast to the other buildings, the palace of Prince Nikita.

My sketch represents the view from the hotel—for Cettinje now possesses this luxury.

The winged house in the centre is the palace. On the right is the Bishop's residence and cathedral, if this term can be applied in this case. In the background is the well-known tower on which the heads of slain Turks were wont to be stuck on spikes, exposed to the jeers of the populace. The present Prince has put an end to this practice and has constructed a wooden belfry on its summit, in which is a large bell, only rung in cases of great emergency, when the hillsmen are to be suddenly called in order to repel some more perilous foray than usual from beyond the border. Cettinje is built in a broad plain, not over fertile, surrounded by lofty hills. This is not the richest plain in Montenegro; but considering what a desert of stones this country for the most part is, it appears a very well favoured spot indeed to the mountaineers.

The legend says that the Almighty, when he distributed stones over the earth, accidentally upset the bag which contained them over Montenegro. It truly looks like it—a more desolate and barren region it is difficult to find: a desert of broken masses of limestone piled one on the other in fantastic heaps. Its character is expressed in the names given it by its neighbours. Montenegro in Italian, Karatag in Turkish, Tchernagora in Sclav, all have the same meaning— The Black Mountain.

As a Montenegrin told me, "This is a poor, rocky country of ours: we produce but two things —fighting men and flea-powder."

This insecticide of Montenegro, made of a certain rock-plant, is renowned all over the East, and is largely exported. It is very efficacious, and well bears out the dogma so impressed upon us in our youth, that bountiful Providence ever finds the antidote where she gives the evil. "The nettle and the dock grow side by side."

The hotel is the finest building in the capital after the palace. It belongs to the Prince, who, observing that inquisitive tourists were beginning to visit his realm, bethought him of this good speculation. He has placed a sergeant of his army in it as manager.

On entering it we were ushered into a comfortable room, not by a smiling chamber-maid, but by a gigantic barbarian bristling with arms.

We sat down and rested for an hour, discussing our plans.

Here we were at last, in the capital of the warlike little State of which the world has heard so much of late—a State which has been belauded far and wide; a State whose fierce sons Mr. Gladstone speaks of in such warm terms, as very far the bravest, noblest warriors of modern Europe; a State which has for so many hundreds of years successfully withstood the Turk in many a heroic battle; but which now, spoiled by too much praise, petted by the rest of Europe, swollen with pride, dreams of aggrandizement at the expense of Turkey, and nurses vast and ambitious projects, in which the central idea is—Cettinje the capital, Prince Nikita the king, of a vast confederacy of the Southern Sclavs.

The Austrian occupation of Herzegovina and Bosnia was naturally very displeasing to the Montenegrins, crushing several of their grand hopes. That Montenegro for years carried on intrigues in the Herzegovina, incited the Christian population to revolt, and encouraged them to look forward to the day when they should be subjects of Prince Nikita, is notorious. The Principality was ever a place of refuge for Herzegovinian fugitives; and, as my readers know, lent valuable assistance in that last insurrection which ended in a great European war.

In the late war Montenegro was very successful, as we all know. Her troops on several occasions defeated the Turks with great slaughter.

It is true that her foemen were not of the first line, but starving, shoeless, demoralized Redifs. However that may be, the representatives of the Powers, at the Congress of Berlin, considering that the prowess and success of her armies merited some recompense, handed over to her a large slip of Turkish territory, giving her what she had so long coveted, a seaport—Antivari.

Her new territory has proved rather troublesome to her, a not unalloyed good. The inhabitants of it do not approve of being thus unceremoniously handed over to the hated Karatags, and offered—and are, I shall have to show by and by, still offering—a formidable resistance to the Prince's troops. As I am on the subject, I may state that the wise men at Berlin made a very serious mistake when they drew a line across the map, to represent the new frontier.

In the first place, whereas it would have been easy to have handed over lands to Montenegro which are inhabited by co-religionists of hers, who would have welcomed their new masters, it was thought fit to give her districts and villages inhabited by the most fiercely fanatical Mohammedans of Albania. That bloodshed and future troubles would result, any one who knew the country could have foreseen. I shall have a good deal more to say on this subject when I get to

Albania. The fact of the matter is, there is no reliable map of this country, so the representatives at Berlin worked in the dark, confused between the utterly contradictory description of the region given by Turkish and Montenegrin envoys.

A good story is told, illustrative of the geographical knowledge of some members of the congress. A noble English representative was conversing with one of the Turkish representatives. He had recently been studying the map of this coast.

"Now," said he, "look here. This little Montenegrin difficulty must be settled. They want a sea-port; give them one: let them have Cattaro."

"We have no objection to that," replied the Turk with a smile, for he knew that the port in question belonged to Austria.

The Englishman was delighted. He went straight to his Austrian colleague. "Ah, the Montenegrin difficulty is settled," he said. "All is smooth now; the Turks have given in."

"I am glad of that. What, then, is proposed?"

The amusement of the Austrian can be imagined when he heard that the Turks had no objection to giving up an Austrian fortress to Prince Nikita.

A frontier commission was sent over last spring to mark out definitely the new boundary-line. It was composed of course of representatives of all the Powers interested. I heard, from several people I met, of the sufferings and difficulties of this much-to-be-pitied expedition. To draw out any frontier-line based on the instructions they had received was hopeless.

At last, about two months before our arrival, a melancholy troop might have been seen descending the rough track that leads from Cettinje to Rieka. The gates of the heavens were opened. The path was converted into a foaming torrent. They reached Rieka wet and miserable. The commissioners then retired to bed and hot beverages, fearful of fever and rheumatism.

At last a happy thought struck one. "The rainy season is commencing. We must postpone our labours till next spring. Let us return to our wives and families."

The English commissioner alone held out, and urged that they should continue their work now. He told them that the rainy season was a good two months off yet. In vain ; the others had had enough of it; they threw up the sponge. The commission broke up. What excuse was made to the several Powers that had sent it out, I know not, but the real cause was a rain-storm on the Montenegrin hills.

The English commissioner was much admired by the populace, and made himself by far the most popular of the lot. He was a good foot taller than any other member of the expedition, and looked like a fine man, as well as a *diplomat*, for so every one is called here who works for a foreign government. He was attended, as far as I could make out, by two smart non-commissioned officers of the line, also big and imposing. One of these thought it incumbent on him to sport a fez at Scutari, which at once stamped the English branch of the commission as Turcophil.

We were aroused suddenly by a loud barbaric shout, not much resembling the cheers of an English crowd.

The Duke of Wittemburg had arrived, so we walked down the high street to see his reception. The whole of the capital had turned out—a picturesque mob, every man of which bristled with arms. The Albanian or Montenegrin never leaves his doorstep without buckling on a very arsenal of formidable-looking weapons. The women, of whom some were pretty, mixed freely with the throng. These wear the same sleeveless white coats as the men do, but no sash ties it in at the waist. Under this is a many-hued dress or petticoat of thick and rough material, which falls some six inches or more below the coat. Their legs are wrapped in shapeless gaiters. They wear the opunka on their feet. They are fond of stringing small Turkish coins, half-piastres and the like, with which they ornament their heads and breasts. Some of the necklaces constructed with the small silver coins are really very pretty.

About 200 men or more were drawn up along the road-side, near the palace, who fired a salute as the *cortége* arrived. Some Montenegrin nobles, in their extravagantly gorgeous dress, mounted on small wiry horses, rode hither and thither, giving orders to the men. Fine specimens, of guerilla chieftains they were, all of great height, handsome, and sinewy.

Very characteristic of this country was it to see the men fall into their places. A gun was fired—the signal that the duke and his party had been sighted in the pass. Then all down the high-street you might see tobacconist, leather merchant, and baker, leap from his counter or leave his work, seize his rifle—always at hand, and always loaded—and run down to the palace gate, where he would take up his position with his fellows in the line. The discipline seemed rather slack, but the strict discipline of a European army would be useless for these men, trained to fighting from their childhood as they are, and who never or rarely descend to the plain to join battle with regular troops, but fight behind the rocks and stones they know so well.

Montenegro has no regular paid army. Every man is a soldier in time of war. Prince Nikita telegraphs his orders to the various *Voyades* or chieftains, and each of these calls out the fighting men of his district. It requires but little time to mobilize these wild forces.

There is no commissariat to be organized, no heavy transport train.

Each man buckles on his belt of cartridges, throws his plaid over his shoulders, seizes his rifle, and stalks out of his door, ready for the campaign. The women take the place of the commissariat. Each man's wife, or mother, or sister, as the case may be, is his commissariat. The women come and go between home and camp, bearing provisions and ammunition. For the particular nature of the service required of the Montenegrins this system is perfect; for they never carry war beyond their frontiers, and the distance between home and the front is never very great. No less hardy than the men, the women here are surprisingly active and strong, and walk nimbly across these fearful mountains with incredibly heavy burdens on their backs.

We dined at the table-d'hôte of the Prince's hotel to-day, in very aristocratic company.

The highest officers of the little State are regular *habitués* of the hotel dinner.

We sat down with the court painter—a young Ragusan who had travelled in America and France, and spoke a curious English, with a half foreign, half American accent, freely larded with Yankee idioms; our landlord; the Secretary of State, the Minister of Foreign Affairs, and the Prince's adjutant.

The latter is a handsome young fellow, a cousin of the Prince, and with him has been educated at the Lycée St. Louis le Grand, at Paris. All the grandees were in full Montenegrin dress, bristling with pistols and yataghans; for in Montenegro the men do not put by their weapons when in a friendly house, as is the case in Albania.

The conversation turned on politics. Mr. Gladstone, of course, was their hero. They were all well acquainted with his pamphlet, which has been translated into their tongue. The hatred they expressed for Lord Beaconsfield was intense. They were by no means reserved in the terms of their abuse.

There was one thing that excited their astonishment to a great degree. "You Englishmen," said one, " Christians—civilized—a great people! How comes it that you allow a Jew to govern you?"

Seeing that we were not quite of one mind with them, and were not such great admirers of Holy Russia as were they, they politely turned the conversation.

We then got on the subject of the perpetual wars on the Turkish frontier, which in ferocity and romantic incident excel the old feuds of our Northern border-land.

A man happened to enter the room while we dined. Our landlord introduced him to us as a very brave fellow, who had cut off twenty-three heads in one battle of the late war, and who, in consideration of his prowess, had received a medal from the hands of the White Czar.

From cut-off heads and noses we got on the subject of Prince Nikita. His praises were loudly sung. This autocrat is greatly beloved by his people. He is a handsome man, tall and powerfully built; married to a very lovely Montenegrin. That the Prince has done much for his country is certain. He has succeeded in abolishing many of the more barbarous customs of his subjects.

Quarter is now given in war by the Montenegrins; and though the mutilation of captured and dead foemen is practised as of old, yet the Turkish heads are no longer bought by the bishop prince at so much a head, to be exhibited on the tower which overlooks the capital.

In the good old times, if you paid a friendly call on the late Metropolitan, a genial kind old gentleman, it was quite a common thing to have your conversation and coffee interrupted by the unceremonious entrance of some wild fellow staggering under the weight of a heavy sack. "Ah! good, good, my son!" the old prelate would say, with sparkling eyes. "How many of them?"

The man would then empty the bag on the floor. Its ghastly contents would be numbered, and the price of blood paid over. The heads would be raked up again and carried off to the tower, then the conversation would be quietly resumed where it left off.

Brigandage is now unknown in Montenegro, for the Prince has done all he could to make his country respectable and of good fame throughout Europe.

His subjects have the reputation of being great pilferers.

The Draconic laws of the country punish this offence with hanging. The Prince has lately mitigated the penalty to whipping. In the eyes of his children this is a still more horrible punishment.

A whipped Montenegro is worse than dead—disgraced—outraged—an outcast on the earth. Many who have been condemned to the whipping have been known to fall down at the Prince's feet and pray to him for mercy—for death—death with torture, rather than the great infamy.

A Montenegrin whipping is no joke; so severe is it, that death often follows the punishment.

I must say, in justice to this people, it is not on that account that the penalty is so dreaded. For like his neighbour the Albanian, the Montenegrin is indifferent to death or physical suffering. He is indeed perfectly brave.

Dinner completed—a much better dinner, I may add, than any Dalmatian hotel can afford—we retired to the adjoining café, in which was a very inferior billiard-table. The room was full of armed Montenegrins, smoking and raki-drinking, a wild-looking crew. It is to be feared that so civilized a luxury as a café and billiard-table must lead many young Montenegrin gentlemen into dissipated habits.

Here—playing together for pots of Austrian beer—were the Minister of Finance, the Prince's adjutant, the innkeeper, the postman, and the pot-boy. In what metropolis, even of the most democratic republic, would one meet with such fraternizing equality as in this little absolute despotism of Montenegro? It was an exceedingly funny sight. All the players were terribly in earnest—quiet and stern over their game.

CHAPTER VI.

The occupation of a Montenegrin gentleman—The public library — Prince Nikita's prisoners — Albanian *versus* Montenegrin—A Montenegrin loan—The Prince as a sportsman —The museum—The hospital.

THE next morning we rose betimes, to visit the lions of the Montenegrin capital.

It struck us, as it strikes most travellers in this country, that the favourite occupation of a Montenegrin in time of peace is to swagger about in peacock fashion in conspicuous places where he is likely to be seen, proud of his fine dress and splendid weapons, which he sticks ostentatiously in his silken sash. The women do work hard here, but I have never seen a Montenegrin of the sterner sex demean himself by any labour. They are all gentlemen, in the good old sense of the word. They can't do any work, and wouldn't if they could.

There is no industry of any kind in this country. Their embroidered robes, their metal work, their saddlery, all come from Albania, or are here worked by emigrants from that province.

The Black Mountaineers have many virtues, but, *pace* Mr. Gladstone, industry is not one of them.

How they manage to procure their expensive get-up often puzzled me. True, all the riches of the country are on the not over-clean backs of the inhabitants.

Miserably poor the common people are. A bad season, as this one has been, equals in horror and suffering even what Ireland has just experienced. Yet a Montenegrin, be he starving, can always manage to be well armed, and often gay with gold embroidery.

We met a string of women, some by no means ill-favoured, bearing building materials—wood, bricks, and the like—on their broad shoulders. They had brought these all the way from Cattaro. As all the luxuries, and many of the necessities of life, have to be brought up that frightful path on the backs of the fair sex, Cettinje is by no means a cheap place to live in. It made my eyes open to learn the cost of a feed of hay for one's horse.

We walked up the high street, till we reached an institution of which the natives are very proud—the public library.

This was but a small room. The books were

few in number, all in the Sclav tongue. I was surprised to find the chief Russian, German, French, and Italian journals lying on the table. There was a *Standard* and *Illustrated London News* of as recent a date as September the 27th.

The Prince, who of course is consulted as to what publications are to be admitted into his realm, has curiously enough selected from our daily papers the one that, above all others, takes a view of general European politics diametrically opposed to that of himself and his big ally in the North.

The next object of interest we visited was the prison. Imagine a courtyard open on the street, generally, I believe, unguarded. Here all offenders against the law squat on the ground, or stroll about as they like. They are allowed to receive their friends, who bring them little luxuries. A most happy-go-lucky sort of a prison, and very characteristic of the country. These prisoners, were they so inclined, could escape in a moment. They never attempt such a thing. They are ordered to remain there and consider themselves prisoners for so many days, and there they stay, smoking patiently till their time is up.

In so small a country as Montenegro, it is hardly an exaggeration to say that everybody knows everybody. The flight of a prisoner would be telegraphed to every village—he would soon be re-captured. For so great is the love and fear entertained by this people towards their Prince, that none would venture to shelter or assist a runaway from his prison. Again, to fly across the frontier is a plan few would care to resort to. The Montenegrin loves his country too much to desert it, and is too much disliked by his neighbours to expect to be by them received with open arms.

The Prince had occasion to send an important message to Cattaro one winter. Heavy snow rendered the path dangerous—almost impracticable. So, as it was a pity to risk the life of an honest man, a criminal from the prison was called out, and ordered to carry the letter to the Austrian fortress, and return immediately. No one for a moment suspected that the man, having regained his liberty, would stay away for good. Indeed, he carried out his mission safely, and returned within two days.

While we were lunching with the grandees in the hotel, several loud explosions, succeeding each other in rapid succession, shook the house to its foundation. We were told that the noise proceeded from the new road to Cattaro, where the rock is being blasted with dynamite. We went out to see the sight. The plain at the back of the hotel was crowded with groups of men, women, and children, who seemed pleased and excited at the spectacle. Every now and then from the rocky ridge, about half a mile off, would spout a huge volume of smoke and fragments of rock, which was followed shortly by a loud roar.

The recklessness of the spectators was amazing. A fragment of rock would fall in the midst of them occasionally, which called forth peals of laughter. They would all rush up to see how deep it had forced its way into the soil. One large piece of rock whizzed by us and buried itself near the hotel, not ten yards from where we were standing, and almost between the legs of a little boy. The urchin screamed with joy (as did all round—the narrow shave was an excellent joke), and threw himself on the ground to disinter what had so nearly proved his destruction. The stone was nearly as large as a man's head, and had buried itself quite eighteen inches in the ground—a sufficiently formidable missile. We were told that a rock had been projected into the Prince's palace the other day during the blasting operations, and that several people had been killed or seriously wounded at different times. The Black Mountaineer is too accustomed to scenes of carnage to be anything but reckless and careless of life.

In the afternoon we saw the Prince himself, as he enjoyed the fresh air of the plain. He was walking in a slow and dignified manner, followed closely by two attendants. He wore the national costume; over his shoulders was thrown a magnicent cloak of furs. Whichever way he turned his head, and he did so often, every one within radius of his vision immediately uncapped himself, and as instantly resumed his head-covering when his sovereign's eyes were turned in another direction again. On no other occasion does the Montenegrin doff his cap; this mark of respect is due to the Prince alone. He wears it indoors as well as out.

Here a man salutes his equal with a kiss on the cheek, his superior with a kiss on the hand or hem of the garment, according to the rank. Woman, an inferior and subject being, never ventures to do more than humbly take in her own, even her husband's, hand and kiss it.

We did not have an interview with Prince Nikita, though we had letters of introduction for him. As he was entertaining the Austrian Grand Duke, we considered that he had enough distinguished foreigners on his hands for one time. Later on Robinson and Jones did interview him, and were much pleased with his frank and genial manner. He is always very glad to see any strangers that visit his domains, and is anxious that his endeavours to civilize and ameliorate the condition of his people should be better known and appreciated by England.

I fear that he and his people have been almost too highly appreciated of late. Some would persuade us that the Montenegrins are the finest people in Europe—a race of Demigods. The popular superstition as to the "unspeakable Turk" is no less absurd than that which exaggerates the virtues of the noble Montenegrin.

They are brave warriors. They are cunning enough to know that the good opinion of civilized Europe is worth having. They are intensely self-conceited; they hate the Turk and the Albanian; they are too proud of their warlike qualities to care to work; and, in my humble opinion, will never be more than they are now, picturesque, poor mountaineers, very inferior in mental capacity to their neighbours the Albanians, Christian or Mohammedan, and no wit less ferocious and cruel in war.

But Albania has an ill-name among those who know her not. She is the scapegrace of the Eastern Adriatic—the cause of all troubles hereabouts, it is said. Montenegro, on the other hand, enjoys a high reputation.

This is natural. Subsidized or bribed by two of the Powers that be, petted by the same, she plays a good game, and encourages the superstition that she is much more virtuous and civilized than the neighbour whose territory she lusts after.

A Montenegrin Loan.

The unfortunate Arnaut has no Prince Nikita, is robbed by the so-called government of Turkey when it is strong enough to affect him in any way, has no friends, but is surrounded by cunning enemies, hungry for his lands.

Let any disinterested person travel among Montenegrin and Arnaut, and I think he will conclude, as I did, that the latter is as brave a warrior—more industrious, more intellectual—in every way of a finer, nobler race, than his much belauded hereditary foe.

The cares of State lie not heavily on the shoulders of Prince Nikita. The little work he does do he is very proud of. Europeans that have conversed with him have come away with the impression that he is the hardest-working, most conscientious prince in Europe.

I am told that now that he has constructed a very complete network of telegraph wires throughout his realm, he considers that one thing alone remains to bring Montenegro up to his standard of civilization.

This is a National Debt. He talks seriously of negotiating a loan in some of the European capitals, and proposes to hypothecate the timber of the State forests. We saw a good deal of Montenegro in this and in a later visit; but had great difficulty in discovering where these fine forests were. We often made inquiries.

"Ah! when you reach So-and-so, you will see them on your right hand." So-and-so reached, we could perceive nothing but the eternal stones of the Karatag, made further inquiries, and were referred to some further spot where we should find huge primeval forests darkening mountain and valley, the haunts of wild beasts, where the axe of the woodman had never been heard to resound, where twenty men linked hand-in-hand would fail to encircle the gigantic trunks.

We pursued these phantom forests, but never found them, so we concluded that they existed only in the imaginations of the Montenegrin financiers.

At last, it is true, on the frontier, near Klementi, we did come across what might be called forests, but the timber was not large; and, growing where it did, in inaccessible haunts of the eagle, in the heart of the wild mountains, it was next to useless.

I should say that if the Principality endeavoured to raise a loan on the security of her inexhaustible stones, she would be about as successful as she will be if she seriously tries to hypothecate her forests.

A rather cynical person, a foreigner, who knows Cettinje well, gave me an amusing summary of Prince Nikita's method of passing his time. In the morning he sits in his palace; occasionally sends a message of little import to some village *Voyade*, through the medium of his new toy, the "electric telegraph." A few telegrams constitute a hard day's work for the Prince. Some relaxation is necessary. Sport is suggested; so off he rides, with his Court, to Rieka, in whose stream are trout of fabulous size. Here he enjoys a good afternoon's fishing. With rod and fly? No; but in a more wholesale and princely fashion. With dynamite! Truly a royal pastime! He is also a poet in his way, and turns out rather dismal compositions in his native tongue. He is an affectionate husband, and is wont, on fine evenings, to serenade the princess with the one-stringed guzla, or violin of Montenegro, accompanying it with his voice, which he raises in song of his own making.

A Montenegrin notable, a fine young fellow, quite six feet five inches in height, kindly offered to be our guide over a Museum of great interest, which is situated at the further extremity of the town. The Museum is merely a small, rough-plastered room, but it contains what is well worthy of visit—a collection of trophies taken from the Turk in those wars which have raged fiercely and cruelly between the two races for so many hundreds of years. Here were the spoils of a thousand battles. Guns of very antique date—curious, ricketty weapons of Middle Age Europe.

Here the long Albanian gun, with silver-inlaid barrel, and small narrow stock of beautifully carved steel; old muskets with English Tower marks; Martini-Henry and Winchester rifles hung on the walls, bringing one down to more recent campaigns. Sabres, blood-stained and broken; mountain howitzers, tattered standards, some falling to pieces with age, some rent with ball and shell; the richly inlaid scimetars of some old Prince of Orient, lances, old chain-armour, and I know not what besides, lay in confusion all around us.

In one corner of the wall hung certain trophies which are calculated to sadden the English visitor. These are the decorations of the slain Turk. Among the Medjidiés were numerous Crimean medals, English and French. It was not pleasant to see these here at Cettinje, taken as they were from the breasts of many a veteran ally of ours in the olden time—heroes of Kars, may be; soldiers of Williams.

From this melancholy collection we were taken to see the Hospital. The surgeon, a Herzegovinian by birth, kindly showed us over the establishment. It was a rough place, but answered its purpose well enough. The beds were occupied chiefly by those who had been badly wounded in the late war. The patients were crowded together in a way that would have much astonished an English doctor. But these hardy, temperate people, have marvellous constitutions, and the air of Cettinje is pure and bracing; so no ill has resulted so far, from a system which would invite pyæmia, and kill off half the inmates of a London hospital in a week.

We stayed at Cettinje for three days. By that time we had seen enough of the metropolis, so held a council as to whither next we should bend our steps.

As Albania, and not Montenegro, was the object of this expedition, we decided to cross the frontier to Scutari, the capital of North Albania, where resided an English and other consuls, who could give us useful information.

We found the best, indeed the only, way of reaching Scutari from here was to go by land to Rieka, a Montenegrin village on the river of the same name, and then hire a boat to take us down the Rieka, and across the great lake of Scutari, to the Albanian capital, which is situated at its furthest extremity.

CHAPTER VII.

Journey to Scutari—Atrocities—A runaway—The vale of Rieka—A Montenegrin sailor—The lions of Rieka—The perils of the night.

We left Cettinje early on a sunny, fresh October morning. Our baggage was strapped on the back of one of the sturdy little horses of the country, which was led by a diminutive native, not twelve years of age, yet armed with yataghan and loaded revolver. His father—a tall, fine fellow, who came to see us off—had been subjected to a horrible mutilation. His nose had been cut off by the Albanians, taking with it the whole upper lip, giving him a ghastly appearance. One meets with an astonishing number of men who have been victims of this barbarous custom. The Montenegrins are quite as great offenders in this respect as are their Albanian foemen. Indeed, I came across more mutilated men in Scutari alone than in all Montenegro.

In the last war, a handsome young Montenegrin was taken prisoner by the Turks. As he was wounded, he was sent to the hospital at Scutari. Some of the ladies of the different consulates, who were doing all that lay in their power to alleviate the sufferings of the wounded, took great interest in this interesting young man. A curious and most offensive smell was noticed at his bedside; it increased, day by day, till it became quite unsupportable. At last its origin was discovered. Rolled up in his coat, which lay by his side, were eighteen Turkish noses!—the tokens of his valour in the field.

Our Montenegrin friends were not pleased to hear that we were going to Albania. "Stay with us," they said; "travel in our country. There is more to see than in Turkey. You will like us. Those beasts of Albanians will cut your throats of a certainty, devils that they are." But we wished to hear the other side of the question, and notwithstanding the warnings of our hosts, determined to visit the "beasts" and "devils," and form our own opinion about them.

A crowd of wild-looking mountaineers had assembled to see us off. We had scarcely got under weigh when an amusing incident happened. Our pack-horse, exhilarated by the fine fresh air of the morning, and a hearty breakfast, thought that a nice canter across the plain of Cettinje would be a pleasant way of beginning the day. So off he went at a canter over the low stone walls, across the potato-fields, through the dried torrent-beds, in a direction quite opposite to that which his *compagnons de route* had chosen. It must have been a ridiculous sight. First a saddle-bag fell off his back, then he would throw a blanket off, until our properties lay scattered all over the plain. We followed as fast as we could with our heavy boots and rifles. We at last caught him, readjusted our baggage, and once more turned his head to the mountain, where soon the narrow and precipitous path obviated all chance of his repeating the performance.

I was smoking a cigarette at the time of the mishap, and swallowed it by accident as I leaped over a wall. The result was an unwonted silence and solemnity on my part for the next half-hour or so.

I was much struck by the behaviour of our guide and the other Montenegrins, when the refractory horse was captured.

English carters, under the same circumstances, would have given vent to much foul language, and would probably have brutally belaboured the wretched animal. But these Montenegrins showed no sign of impatience, said not a word, but quietly repacked the horse and led it off. Turks, Albanians, Montenegrins, and all Easterns, whatever their other faults, are very good to the dumb animals that serve them, and never ill-treat them.

To shoot any animal wilfully, for the mere sake of killing, excites great indignation in the breast of an Albanian. An English naturalist, who travelled in their country in order to make a collection of birds, was looked upon as something not much better than a devil. His very servant was so horrified at the wholesale massacre of the innocents carried on by his master, that he gave him notice that he could serve such a fiend no longer, and left him on the spot. Yet these are the very people who feel no compunction in blowing your brains out from behind a fence, in satisfaction of some trifling quarrel.

It is an easy morning's march to Rieka. The rough path first ascends the rocky ridge which divides the plain of Cettinje from the valley of Rieka (Rieka = river). When we reached the summit of this ridge a most magnificent scene opened out before us.

The great valley lay at our feet. From the windy desolate height on which we stood we saw far beneath the silver stream of the Rieka, fringed with poplars, winding down a long fertile vale. From the edge of the water-side meads the great mountains rose sheer up on either side—of every form and colour—some barren, in curious strata which shone in the morning sun like successive rings of opal and Parian marble, others covered with woods, that had already assumed their autumn tints, and sent forth a perpetual moan as the strong highland wind passed over them.

From the lofty eminence on which we stood chain was seen rising over chain, valley behind valley, till, far away behind all, there gleamed a long broad sheet of water, the great lake of Scutari, backed by the fantastic-shaped rugged mountains of Albania, utterly barren, serrated and pinnacled like a gigantic gothic cathedral, and through the medium of the clear southern atmosphere appearing of a delicate pinkish hue.

This valley of Rieka is far the most fertile of Montenegro, and the village of the same name which is situated on the brink of the clear stream is the prettiest, cleanest, and seemingly most prosperous of the country.

The extreme smallness of some of the fields, if they can be so called, which is remarkable all over Montenegro, struck us much, on our descent down the rough slopes of the mountain.

Soil is scarce. We here saw walled enclosures so small that three or four potato-plants at the most filled them up. Our procession entered Rieka about mid-day. This village consists of one street along the river side. The houses are built tastefully of wood, something in the Swiss style. Outside each house was the usual stone bench, on which, again, as usual, half the family sat, smoking lazily, evidently with nothing on earth to do. Of course we were inspected with some curiosity as we passed.

Not understanding the language, we were utterly at the mercy of our guide. We tried to signify to him that we wished him to conduct us to a *khan*. He shook his head, and paid no other attention to our remarks, but deliberately marched us off to the establishment which he thought was alone suitable for the English *Gospodinas*. It was the largest house in the place, whitewashed, and partly hanging over the water, at the corner of the pretty bridge which spans the stream.

We halted at the foot of the stone steps which led up to the door, and unpacked our horse; while the crowd stood round, admiringly, and whispering to our guide queries as to what these curious strangers might be.

The door of the house opened, and a pleasant-looking old lady, richly-attired, and tinkling at every motion with the strings of Turkish coins which she wore as ornaments, came down smiling, bowed low to us, kissed our hands, and invited us within. We were soon made at home, and a welcome repast of wheaten cakes and goats' flesh was placed before us, with good *raki* to wash it down.

The captain of the village came in while we were lunching—a splendid-looking fellow, who stalked in with the magnificent carriage which distinguishes the chieftains of *Tchernagora*. He approached us with both hands stretched out, and shook us cordially by the hands, and gave us what was evidently a very kindly welcome, in words we unfortunately could not understand. A few other men of rank came in to see us, but none could speak any language but their own, so our conversation was limited to smiling welcomes on the one hand, and smiling thanks on the other. We all found that this after a time became monotonous, so we endeavoured to render the interview a little more amusing by a mutual inspection of weapons.

After lunch a room was prepared for us. This was by far the most civilized mansion we came across in Montenegro. There were actually beds in it. Such a luxury was quite unknown a few years ago in this country.

The Montenegrin never takes his clothes off. On retiring for the night, he merely rolls himself up in his plaid, and lies down on the bare floor of his house.

A shake, and then an inspection and buckling on of arms, suffice for his toilette in the morning. We were sketching the village after lunch, when a man passed us, stopped, looked at us a moment curiously, and then, to our astonishment and delight said, "You should be Englishmen, strangers."

This man turned out to be a Montenegrin, who had once got somehow to Constantinople. Here he shipped on board an English brig, and so had visited London, Liverpool, and other ports. It is a question whether a Montenegrin had ever before adopted the sea as a profession, it is hardly in the line of the Karatag, detesting as he does discipline and confinement of any kind.

He was known as Greek Jack on board the brig, he told us. English sailors I have always found, have rather a vague idea as to the limits of the little realm of King George. Any one who has a cut-throat appearance, and is picked up anywhere between Dalmatia and Cyprus, is at once looked upon by our tars as one of them blank Greek chaps. His English was scanty, but rich at any rate in every foullest oath our seaports can teach the foreign visitor.

Nearly every other word was an emphasis of this nature. From him we learnt that the house we occupied belonged to the prince. He himself was now a hand on board the prince's steam-yacht, a very small vessel, in which the great Nikita is wont to travel on the Lake of Scutari, when on a dynamite fishing expedition.

Our new friend kindly offered to act as our guide if we wished to do the lions of Rieka.

These consisted of two little public-houses, one famous for its wine, the other for its raki. We did them; the result was that our cicerone's English became more and more indistinct, but at the same time more and more larded with profanity, till gradually, from every other word, two out of every three words at least, were oaths. Had there been one more lion to be done, I verily believe that every word of his conversation would in our country have rendered him liable to that small pecuniary penalty which our statutes inflict in such cases.

Raki and mastic, the favourite beverages of this part of Europe, are drinkable: that is all that can be said for them.

Raki is a colourless spirit, extracted from the skins of grapes after the wine-making. It is not nice, but is, I should say, pure and wholesome.

Mastic is extracted from mountain herbs, tastes like absinthe, and is probably nearly as poisonous.

This was a night of tribulation for Brown.

Our room swarmed with the far-famed Montenegrin fleas, and other still more ferocious natives. The ramparts of insecticide with which he surrounded himself availed nought. Sleep he knew not.

In the dead of night I was suddenly awakened by the utter collapse of the wooden bed on which I slept. It fell to pieces without any warning, and precipitated me on the floor.

Stories I had read in Christmas Annuals of robber inns, and traps that opened out in floors to swallow up the sleeping traveller, flashed across my brain. But there was no occasion for alarm. On lighting a match and inspecting the ruins, I came to the conclusion that the bed had been undermined by vermin—that was all.

CHAPTER VIII.

A great victory—A good old custom—On the Lake of Scutari—The londra—The debateable land—Boat song—Encampment—Scutari—A reminiscence of Cremorne—The brothers Toshli—Willow-pattern plates—At the British Consulate.

The next was a glorious morning. We were up at daybreak, and with the assistance of our friend, bargained with four men to take us in a boat to Scutari.

The captain of the village also came to our aid, and beat down the rather exorbitant demands of his countrymen.

The captain was evidently an important personage—to be respected and feared; for the fellows ceased their vehement jabbering, and became very humble and quiet, when he appeared on the scene.

Our nautical friend told us that this *Voyade* was a distinguished warrior. He had been engaged in that great victory gained over the Turks in 1858.

Some of my readers may remember that in that year an army of 6000 Turkish regulars invaded Montenegro. They had advanced some miles up one of those frightful defiles by which alone the Black Mountain is to be penetrated, when they were surprised by a body of Montenegrins, much inferior in numbers, but having the advantage of a thorough acquaintance with every rock and crevice of the grey hills. Of the 6000 Turks, but six men and the commander of the expedition escaped. It was only owing to the intercession of certain of the great powers that the Prince did not follow up this great victory by an invasion of the Herzegovina, where, of course, all the Christians would have flocked to his standard.

An international commission was sent out to definitely settle a frontier-line between Montenegro and Turkey—as vain an undertaking as that of the present year will probably prove to be.

As we knew not how long a voyage lay before us, we laid up a store of provisions in our vessel—the round wheaten cakes of the East, "baken on the coals," probably similar to those the Shunamite placed before Elisha long ago, a gourd of wine with a strong smack of the goat's skin, goat's milk cheese, and an abundance of fine black grapes.

Our boat awaited us some few hundred yards down the stream, where the water was sufficiently deep to float her; for the Rieka is here but a shallow brook. Our boatmen had a good deal of poling and wading to do for the first mile or so, as we were constantly grounding on the shingle banks.

Before leaving, a ceremony had to be observed which prevails all over these countries, and which, like many good old customs, has died out in more civilized countries. Our host tucked a bottle of raki under his arm, and, taking a small glass in his hand, accompanied us to where we were to embark, and then handed round the final stirrup cups in most liberal manner.

The *londra*, as the boat of the country is called, is a roughly-made, flat-bottomed affair, with prow and stern alike—sharp pointed, and running up high out of the water, something like the Venetian gondola. These boats are of every size, from the small cranky tub propelled with one oar, to the lengthy twelve-oared vessel.

They have little beam, and must be exceedingly dangerous on the lake in choppy weather—indeed, accidents often occur; but every one here is so happily careless, and trustful in *kismet*, that these ricketty coffins have not been superseded by any more seaworthy craft.

The *londra* is tarred inside and out; there are no benches; the passengers squat on their blankets at the bottom of the boat. The rowers stand up

THE LONDRA.

IMMORAL.

facing the bow, and force their long clumsy sweeps through the water in short, quick jerks.

They do not make use of rollocks, but twist vine or clematis branches into grommets, which run through holes made for the purpose in the gunwale. These grommets soon wear out, and have to be replaced three or four times in a day's journey. The londra, notwithstanding its rough build, progresses at a very fair pace, so long as it does not meet with a strong head-wind, when its little hold on the water is much against it.

Having comfortably settled ourselves at the bottom of our vessel, among our blankets and saddle-bags, we bid adieu to our sailor friend with an *au revoir* in London, when he should next visit that port, and got under weigh. Our crew consisted of four brigand-like Montenegrins, who were dirty and miserable, in all save their weapons, which were beautiful. One was the proud possessor of a long pistol, with a silver hilt inlaid with precious stones, the spoil of the Turk. Each had his gun with him, so we were a formidable-looking party.

The banks of the Rieka are exceedingly fine; rocks and dense foliage on either side, with occasional glimpses of the great mountain behind.

Where the river broadened into the lake we rowed through large fields of waterlilies in full bloom. The country seemed altogether uninhabited. We passed one or two londras, whose crews entered into animated discourse with our men, evidently anxious to know who the European travellers might be. At last we were on the great lake. On all sides it is shut in by lofty mountains, some, I should say, quite 10,000 feet in height. Its surface is studded with numerous bare rocky islands, uninhabited by man, but noisy with multitudes of wild fowl and pelicans. Egrets, divers, and ducks, are very numerous on this water. We hugged the western or Montenegrin shore, for the provisions of the Berlin Treaty have given nearly all this side of the lake to the principality.

We were struck by the extreme desolation of the country; gaunt, uncultivated mountains fell to the water's edge. Population there seemed to be none.

Once we saw a village on the shore; on approaching it, it proved to be ruined, deserted—a mere heap of charred débris—a melancholy relic of fierce frontier war. Here, as later on, on the plains of Podgoritza, I noticed that there was a sort of debateable land on the borders of the two countries—a desert region, where men dare not build or cultivate, not knowing when the dogs of war should again be loosed. Thus rich plains are left to the wolf and lynx, the peasant preferring to build his homestead in the poorer but more secure fastnesses of the mountains, than on the rich lowland, where he would sow only that a hostile horde should reap.

As there was a slight breeze, our men hoisted a small square sail, of whose use they seemed to have but little idea. They made fast the sheet and tack to the weather gunwale, and attempted to sail close hauled.

We moved through the water it is true, but astern and to leeward. Much wrangling then ensued as to the proper method of navigating the vessel. Ultimately the crew lowered their canvas in despair, of which we were not sorry, for we very nearly capsized once in a slight squall. Halyard and sheet were securely knotted, and of course the clumsy craft would not come up to the wind.

Had the puff been a little stronger we must have gone down.

Swimming would not have been easy with our heavy accoutrement.

We could not converse much with the men, as our knowledge of Montenegrin was exceedingly limited. We had compiled a little dictionary, with the assistance of our friends at Cettinje. The usual programme of handing tobacco round, examining each other's arms, was gone through.

Brown rather astonished one of the crew; he had taken hold of the fellow's rifle, and wishing to express his approval of it, pointed to it and read out of the dictionary what he thought was Sclav for " good gun," but which on more careful inspection proved to signify " roast mutton."

All day we paddled along the lone shore, but no town was yet in sight. The evening brought with it one of the most magnificent sunset effects I have ever witnessed. The near mountains on our starboard hand assumed a cold dark appearance as the sun set behind them. Their deep barren defiles had a weird bleakness about them, such as one sees in lifeless Arctic landscapes.

But far away on the port hand, across the water, the rays of the setting sun fell full on the great Albanian mountains, which towered behind the broad plain that fringes the eastern shore of the lake.

Every detail of the fantastic peaks and fissures of the barren granite was sharp and distinct in this clear atmosphere.

Where the rock jutted out it was lurid crimson, as of red-hot coal—elsewhere, of lovely rose and golden tints, while the darker shadows of the hollows were of a deep purple or violet. So utterly barren were these great offshoots of the Mount *Scardus*, that under this strange light the scenery was of a peculiarly unearthly and weird nature. One could almost imagine oneself to be gazing at a landscape of some lifeless star—a chaos of molten matter—silent but for the occasional roar of fire and volcanic action.

But the blue shadows soon rose up from the water's edge, till the last highest peak lost its crown of fire, and the fine day was succeeded by a lovely starlit night.

The day had been hot, but now it became intensely cold; the wind, which was right in our teeth, freshened; the ripple that broke on the shingle shore became louder; and soon the surface of the lake was broken into short choppy waves capped with foam, that glistened in the starlight. The water washed occasionally over our bulwarks in ominous splashes.

There was evidently quite enough sea for our frail craft. But our men, though they made little progress against the head-wind, pulled on pluckily, encouraging themselves with a wild barbaric chant, which was caught up now by one, now by another —a monotonous yet energetic song, to which their blades kept time.

One of these boat-songs was afterwards translated to me. It runs something thus (I have preserved to a certain extent the irregularity of the original):—

>Now then, my hawks, pull! pull!
>Let the boat fly over the water!
>The rocks on the shore are full
>Of Arnauts, thirsty for our slaughter.

But we fly swifter than their bullets go.
They cannot take aim, so swift we row.
    Pull! my hawks, pull!

Long before their slow feet can return
We will fall upon their village—sack and burn,
Tear up the smoking rafters of their homesteads
Into torches that shall light our homeward way,
Laden with rich spoil and foemen's heads.
Now then, my hill hawks, pull away!
    Pull! my hawks, pull!

We expected every moment to see the lights of Scutari burst upon us as we rounded some rugged promontory; but hour after hour of the night passed by, and still no sign of human habitations. Suddenly our boatmen rested on their oars, and entered into a short discussion. When they had come to a decision they pointed to the shore, and endeavoured to explain something to us; what, we could not make out. The dictionary we had compiled at Cettinje was a modest work, containing only words of greeting and the names of strict necessities. The next operation of our crew was to run the boat high and dry on the shingle beach; they then disembarked, and beckoned us to follow.

A fire was soon made up with the brushwood and oleander that grew thickly on the bank.

What next? we wondered. Was this merely a halt for a little rest and supper? or had our crew struck work, and determined to camp here for the

SCUTARI FISHING HARBOUR.

Page 109.

night? We soon found out that the latter was their intention; for after we had supped and smoked a few cigarettes, they one by one rolled themselves up in their cloaks and fell asleep, feet to the fire.

We followed their example, and in consequence of our close proximity to the Montenegrins experienced the attacks of vast armies of fleas.

At four in the morning we got under weigh; it was still dark, but the first faint streak of dawn was visible over the eastern hills. We discovered, later on, that we had encamped on the beach till daylight, because all boats are prohibited from approaching Scutari during the night.

Three Turkish gunboats are stationed off the town, by whom we should have been challenged and stopped, had we proceeded.

At about seven in the morning we reached Scutari. First we had to row through a curious fishing village, which is at the junction of the lake and the broad river that here flows into it. A large number of thatched huts, built on piles, form regular streets in the centre of the stream.

Then the town lay before us, with its old Venetian fortress perched on a lofty rock in the back ground.

We were not much struck by the general appearance of the capital of North Albania—a dingy, dilapidated bankrupt sort of a place it seemed to be.

Scutari is built on the flat promontory formed by the river Bojana, which takes off the waters of the lake to the Adriatic, and another river, which flows into the lake after having crossed the spacious plain which lies between Scutari, and the distant mountains of Biskassi.

On landing, no custom-house or custom-house officers were anywhere visible. We paid off our ship, selected a ragged-looking ruffian to carry our luggage, shouldered our rifles, and marched off to the hotel Toshli, at the other end of the straggling town, which had been recommended to us by the gendarme whose acquaintance we had made on the Austrian Lloyd steamer.

Our first impressions of the city were not favourable. It had an appearance of melancholy decay, still trying to keep up an appearance. The mosques, and some of the better Turkish houses, were rather gaudily ornamented with wooden carvings and bright paint; but now the carvings were broken, and the paint half rubbed off. There was a tea-garden-in-liquidation look about the place.

I remember once seeing Cremorne by daylight. It was some time after outraged respectability had closed the gardens; the occasion being a patriotic meeting which was held there, during the Russo-Turkish war. It was a sad sight to one who had known the place in other days. The plaster statues were broken; the pagodas and the other gimcrack edifices were mouldy, tumbling to pieces, and destitute of paint. This melancholy city of Scutari reminded me irresistibly of Cremorne that day. Everything had been allowed to fall into decay. Any repairing of public or private buildings had long been given up by government and people. One rickety mosque was very funny; its steeple was tiled, if I may use the expression, with the sides of paraffin boxes and Huntley and Palmer's biscuit tins.

The rough paintings on its walls were chipped and dim. The very mollah, in his turban and dirty blue robe, who stood at the door, had a dissipated and unkempt appearance, which harmonized with his surroundings.

Our first impressions of the inhabitants were no less unpleasing. There was a haggard, anxious, half-starved expression in the faces of all we met— a savage fierceness in their eyes, which we had not observed in Montenegro. No one besides ourselves was in European costume, but we attracted no attention; all stalked by us with the utmost indifference. Every man we met—kilted Mussulman, or white-clad Arnaut—was armed to the teeth.

It was some way to Toshli's. We passed through many narrow streets, paved in a fashion well calculated to dislocate the ankles, and traversed numerous grave-yards, neglected and filthy in the extreme.

The hotel turned out to be an unpretending sort of an establishment, half grocery, half café. It was kept by two brothers, Greeks from Janina. It was situated in the principal street of the Christian quarter, close to the foreign consulates. Toshli's is a rough free-and-easy sort of place, but is to be recommended. The cuisine was really very fair. It was curious to observe in the grocery how many English commodities were procurable.

On the shelves I saw Huntley and Palmer's biscuits, Cross and Blackwell's pickles, and, most wonderful of all, brown Windsor soap—an article for which I should imagine that there could be no demand in Albania.

One meets with certain English manufactures in the most remote regions of the world.

I have bought Gillot's steel pens in an Arab town in a remote oasis of the Saharah.

Another curious fact is, that here at Toshli's, and everywhere else in Eastern Europe where plates are in use, one invariably meets with our old willow-pattern services. There is a very large exportation of these from England to these countries.

The café of the hotel, in which is a billiard-table,

is much frequented by the Christian merchants, and the Turkish military doctors of the garrison; these are all Christians, being Armenians, Greeks, Poles, and other foreigners.

Italian is understood by many of the Christian merchants here, being the language of commerce on these coasts.

There must, I should say, be a certain amount of Italian blood in the veins of the citizens of Scutari, for it was long one of the strongest Venetian dependencies, and sustained one of the most heroic sieges of history, when Mahomet II. overran Eastern Europe, in the fifteenth century, with his vast hordes of infidels, inflamed with uninterrupted success.

Scutari was finally acquired by Turkey in 1479, by treaty.

The brothers Toshli received us with open arms, for the gendarme had prepared them for our arrival. Having settled ourselves in a comfortable bed-room, which was elegantly draped with strings of malodorous—not to say putrid—sausages, we indulged in some café-au-lait, a luxury we had not enjoyed for some time.

We then called on Mr. Kirby Green, the British consul-general for North Albania, and chargé-d'affaires for Montenegro. This gentleman seemed exceedingly glad to see us, met us with outspread hand, and the remark that " it was rare

I

to see any of his countrymen out here, it was quite an eventful day for him." During our stay in Scutari, Mr. Green did all in his power to assist us in every way. This gentleman, whose experience of Eastern character is very extensive, is emphatically the right man in the right place. It was surprising to find what influence he has in the country, and how excellently he upholds the dignity of England.

He stands very high in the opinion of the natives of both creeds.

"Yes, he is pasha here, and greater than the pasha," was often said of him in my hearing, both by Christians and Mohammedans. They hold him in high respect; and the firmness and justice with which he invariably acts, astonishes and pleases these Orientals, so little accustomed to the like.

Up in the wild mountains, later on, when among the fierce Miridites and Klementis, no sooner did the men we met hear that we were from Scodra (as Scutari is called by the Albanians) and friends of Zutné Green, the savage frown and suspicious handling of yataghan would change to smile of pleasure, and hand outstretched in welcome.

We told Mr. Green what our plans were, and asked him if they were feasible.

We thought of traversing Albania from north to south, from Scutari to the port of Previso, opposite Corfu, by the route of Priserin, Ochrida,

Monastir, and Janina. Mr. Green is not a man to discourage travellers without good cause, but said, "Priserin, let me tell you, is the headquarters of the Albanian League, an organization of the most fanatical Mussulmen of the country, whose object is to resist the Austrian advance, and the Montenegrin claims, by force of arms.

"These men are now worked up to a high pitch of religious zeal, and hatred of the Christians. Priserin is, with perhaps the exception of Mecca, the most dangerous spot for a Christian in all Mohammedan countries. It is true that they may receive you very well, as Englishmen, and entertain you with the greatest hospitality; or they may cut your throats as soon as they see you. It is a toss up which of the two they will do.

"You will be either honoured guests, or abominations to be instantly put to death.

"They are the same men that murdered Mehemet Ali, at Jakova. So I advise you to consider the matter carefully."

As guests at Mr. Green's table, later on in the evening, we received a lot of very useful information as to the state of the country, and the ways and means of travelling through it.

CHAPTER IX.

Condition of Albania—Her races—The Mussulman—The Christian—The Arnaut—Prince Scanderbeg—Turkish rule—Albanian language—Gendarmes on strike—A Scutarine beauty—Courtship and marriage—Nuns.

HAVING now brought my readers into Albania, it does not seem out of place to here give a rough sketch of this almost unknown province of Turkey.

The first thing that strikes one is the utter lawlessness of the people. The Turks have never assimilated their remoter possessions. It is not in their character to do so. They seem, even after so many centuries, to be merely temporarily encamped in Albania. They have pachas and garrisons in the towns, but the natives enjoy a surprising amount of independence, and are allowed to do pretty well as they like. Indeed, the government is very weak here, neither feared nor respected—merely tolerated. The mountain tribes are almost as little under Turkish rule as were the Montenegrins themselves, over whom, until the treaty of Berlin, the Porte claimed a suzerainty. Out of the towns, Turkish officials are not to be found. A powerful tribe will often refuse to pay the *dimes* to the tax farmer, when a bloody and cruel war will probably ensue, lingering on for years in the hills, in which the government troops will often come off the second best.

At the period of our visit, Albania is in a state of positive anarchy—the gendarmerie on strike, the soldiers refusing to salute their officers, neither having received pay for months, while the natives hold seditious meetings publicly, and unmolested, in the mosques of the garrison towns, in which rebellion against the Porte is fearlessly advocated.

Nowhere is the rotten condition and utter helplessness of the Porte more apparent than here.

The natives, though of one race, may be divided into three classes, differing very much in manners and character. First, we have the Albanian Mohammedan. This is the " wild Albanian kirtled to the knee "—in North Albania, found chiefly in the towns. He is the aristocrat, maybe an owner of lands in the mountains, which he lets out to Arnaut tenants, living on his rents. He is intensely proud of his caste, a despiser of his Christian fellow-townsmen. Courteous, gentlemanly, not over strict in the observance of his creed, he will drink raki on the quiet with an easy conscience.

His walk is a haughty stalk. With his gold-embroidered vest, bright sash—his leather pouch in front, in which are stuck two gold-hilted jewelled pistols and yataghan, his many-folded snowy festinelle, or kilt, which swings from side to side as he struts along—he is indeed an imposing-looking figure.

Secondly, we have the Christian town's-man of the Latin Church—how different in every respect! He wears the fez, Turkish jacket, baggy trousers tied in at the knee, followed by white socks, and European elastic-side boots.

As a Christian the law forbids him to carry arms. There is the timid, fawning, insincere look in his face, so characteristic of the oppressed. These Christians are all traders or merchants, many of them wealthy, but not daring to be over ostentatious, for they live in fear and dread of their unscrupulous neighbours of the other creed, who have on more than one occasion pillaged the Christian quarter. Their position is much what that of the Jews was in medieval Europe.

The dress of the Christian town's-women is not becoming, though exceedingly expensive. Their robe is heavy and thick with gold embroidery, which crackles loudly as they walk. Out of doors they are enveloped in a very ugly red cloak: it is baggy and shapeless. Take an egg, paint it red, cut a good slice off one end and stand it up—you will form a very good idea of a Scutarine Christian lady in outdoor costume. As they are veiled, like the Mohammedans, it is equally impossible to judge of the beauty of either face or figure.

Next we have the third class of the population, the most interesting of all, the country people—or rather, mountaineers, for little but mountain is there in North Albania. These are the Arnauts—Skipitars, as they call themselves—a fierce, hardy race of almost savages, independent, unconquered by the Turks. They too are Latin Christians, but how different from their co-religionists in the town! Their features are indicative of minds that would not tolerate slavery. They stalk proudly through the streets of the towns, bristling with arms, notwithstanding the laws which forbid the Christian to do so. These warlike tribes are too strong to heed the regulations of the feeble government. Their dress is simple, but very manly and workmanlike. They are clad in white homespun from head to heel. Their head-dress is a white skull cap; sometimes they twist a long scarf round the head and under the chin, very much in the style of the Bedouin—this is the "shawl-girt head" that Byron speaks of; a white jacket, with tight sleeves reaching to the wrist, of thick woollen stuff, ornamented with black braid here and there; trousers of the same material, and similarly black braided, baggy behind, but thence close fitting to the leg until they reach the ankle, where they are slit and open out—exactly the cut indeed of the nether garments of the American Indian, except that the lower end is of thicker material, and has the appearance of a gaiter, though it is of one piece with the rest of the garment; opunkas on the feet; a sash round the waist, of common red stuff or of silk, according to the wealth of the man; round the waist a belt, with leather pouch in front, in which the long beautifully worked pistols and yataghan are stuck; a belt of Martini-Henry cartridges over the sash, if he own one of these rifles—if not, a belt from which depend quaint elegantly-carved cartridge and oil-rag boxes, of gold or brass, and long tassels of black silk.

Such is the appearance of an Arnaut mountaineer—a grand costume, showing off the supple, erect frame—the very dress for a savage warrior. The Arnaut, like the Mussulman, shaves his head, leaving a little bunch of hair on the scalp. This gives him a very Indian-like and ferocious appearance. No one who has not seen it can form an idea how this shaving increases the savageness of the expression.

The dress of the women is as hideous as that of the men is handsome. It is not unlike that of the Montenegrins. Their heads are swathed in richly-hued shawls. Their dress is of very thick coarse material, and shapeless. They are fond of wearing leather bands round the waist, ornamented with pins, which are thrust through the leather, with their ends bent up, their heads thus forming elegant patterns on the outside. Round the neck and on the dress, the Arnaut belle wears strings of piastres, swanzickers, and other small coins. Her legs are swathed thickly with a sort of gaiter, which completely prevents one from forming any idea as to the shapeliness of her lower limbs. Most of the mountaineers still wear over their shoulders the curious little black cloak, not unlike the tippet which English ladies have recently copied from their coachmen, which was adopted in mourning for the death of the great Albanian hero Scanderbeg, whose exploits are still sung over the wintry fire by many a mountain bard, to the melancholy accompaniment of the mandolin. There is not an Albanian who is not acquainted with his history.

Albania was once an independent Christian country, though paying tribute to the Porte.

John Castrioti was Prince of the mountain fortress of Kroia and the surrounding country. In 1404 a son was born to him, who was christened George. This was the future hero and deliverer of Albania.

The Prince was persuaded to send this son to the court of Murad II. to be educated. Contrary to the promises made to the father, the boy was brought up in the Mohammedan faith, and when old enough he entered the Turkish army.

On the death of Castrioti, Murad seized his dominion, and attempted with fire and sword to convert the people to the true faith. From that time Scanderbeg formed a design to expel the Turk and liberate his countrymen. He swore a great oath in secret, that never till he died would he cease to wage war on the Turk. The opportunity soon came. He entered into a secret agreement with the Hungarians, and with their assistance defeated the Turks at Nissa with great slaughter.

A fierce war, in which no quarter was given, was then commenced between the Albanians and their oppressors. Driven at times into the fastnesses of the mountains; Scanderbeg ever renewed his brave, seemingly fruitless attempt, when occasion offered.

Ultimately he succeeded in driving the Turks out of Albania; he renounced the Mohammedan faith, and established himself on the throne of his fathers.

Even when he lived the deliverer was almost worshipped as a God. He died in 1467. Then the Albanians, deprived of his skilful generalship, were in time subjugated by the Turks.

Prince George Castrioti was without doubt an extraordinary man. The name of Scanderbeg

(Alexander) was given him by the Turks, in their admiration of his prowess.

To say that the Turks have subjugated the Arnauts is not strictly correct. Their position is something like that of the French in the remoter parts of Algeria. They hold certain towns, the intervening country being occupied by independent tribes, governing themselves, having their own laws.

Why, if a Turkish pasha wishes to traverse the mountains through the district of a certain tribe, he must consult the Boulim-Bashi, the town-representative or consul of that tribe, obtain his permission—his safe-conduct—ere he dare undertake the journey.

The administration of criminal law is not a large item of the expenses incurred by the Turkish Government in their rule of Albania. They leave all this to two unpaid judges, who have from time immemorial been the only two dispensers of justice tolerated by the free people—viz., Judge Lynch and Judge Vendetta. Of these I shall have more to say by-and-by.

The Arnauts are divided into several powerful clans, of which the Clementis and the Miridites are the most important in this district. The tribes differ slightly in costume and language. Some tribes, like the Miridites, are in a wretched condition, starving in their mountains, the result of a long protracted war with the government, originating probably in some petty dispute with a tax collector. These wars hang on in a desultory way for years, until the wretched highlanders, in order to support existence, are obliged to become bandits and cattle-lifters—outlaws—the enemies of all men. A Miridite is now a wretched object generally. I have seen them crawl through the narrow alleys of the bazaar of Scutari, ragged, scowling at every one, haggard and weak with hunger, their arms sold for bread —the sign of extreme poverty, for it is a bitter thing for an Arnaut to part with his beloved weapons, heirlooms as a rule. The ramrod of his lost pistols alone dangles from his belt. This, curiously enough, no man ever seems to part with —probably because it is unsalable.

The Albanians are by some supposed to be the descendants of the ancient Pelasgi, and of a far purer race than are the modern Greeks. From the uniformly classic features of the people I should be inclined to adopt this view. The men have splendid skulls, lofty broad brows and small delicately moulded features.

The women are the most beautiful in Eastern Europe. The children are lovely. They have large solemn eyes and splendid mouths—this latter is their most striking feature—slightly turned down at the sides, which gives a singularly sweet and thoughtful expression. One cannot be long among the Arnauts before perceiving that they are evidently of a noble and ancient race, to which the Montenegrin and other Sclav races will bear no compare. The polite manners, the delicacy of perception and tact of these otherwise savage mountaineers, is very pleasant. Fierce and cruel as foes, reckless of life, they yet are splendid friends; faithful—knowing not what treachery is—truthful, virtuous; hospitable, jovial companions, abstemious as a rule, yet not disinclined on grand occasions to pass freely round the cheering raki (a spirit extracted from grape skins after the wine is made) and the absinthe-like mastic.

The language of the Skipitars, as the Arnauts call themselves, varies much in different districts. Old Illyrian probably in origin, it contains Greek, Latin, and Sclavonian words, in almost equal proportion; at least, so it seemed to me, here in the north. For instance, here are the first thirteen numerals in Albanian; the three tongues I mention are all traceable in these—*gui, du, tre, kater, pens, giasct, sctat, téte, nand, deit, gnim-deit, dum-deit, trem-deit.*

The Albanians do not write in Sclav characters as do their northern, nor in Greek as do their southern neighbours, but, unlike all other races hereabouts, use the Latin character. In addition to our twenty-four letters, they have five others, something like, yet differing in form and pronunciation from, certain of the Greek letters.

Such are the inhabitants of the country—a country as wild as they. Well did Byron call Albania " the rugged nurse of savage men."

The Acroceraunian Mountains and the Mount Pindus send their branches across the whole province. Rugged rocks are heaped one upon the other, with summits hidden in the clouds. It is a region of tempests, which, like to Montenegro, is too poor and barren to produce aught but warriors, who seem ever to thrive best on poor soil, as the stately pines do. The products of the country are few. The acorns of the Vallona oak, which are used for dyeing purposes, martin skins, and boxwood, are the only exports; and not much of these finds its way out of the country. The history of Albania would afford much of interest to any one who would study it.

Once included in the great Bulgarian kingdom, then divided into small principalities, Albania was at last, not without much bloodshed, absorbed by her two powerful neighbours—Venice on the north, Turkey on the east. All the valour of Prince Scanderbeg could only delay for one lifetime the subjugation of his beautiful native land.

Our friend the officer of gendarmerie called on us

on the following morning. With him we took a stroll through the town.

He was rather melancholy. He had received no pay for fourteen months, and was commencing to be disgusted with his profession.

His men were in still more wretched plight. Their red uniforms were ragged and torn; many were barefooted. The poor fellows seemed to be all half-starved. At the present moment they were on strike—"en grève," as our friend rather mildly termed what we should call mutiny.

I do not imagine the community loses much by their defection, for the gendarmerie in Albania is a miserable and almost useless body of men. It might fairly be asked what is the good of having police at all in a country where murder and every other crime are recognized institutions? Even rebellion and treason seem not to be punishable offences, for, as I shall have to narrate further on, the Albanian League hold seditious meetings under the very nose of the pashas.

What then have the police to do?

With our friend as cicerone to explain all we saw, we traversed the Christian, and then the Mohammedan quarter of the town.

The streets of the latter are dismal alleys, with lofty walls on either side; for the Mussulman is a person of retiring habits. He loves to build his house, and establish his harem, in the centre of a pleasant garden, which he surrounds with such high walls that no prying eye can spy his conjugal bliss. A semi-detached villa would never suit him. A door in one of these walls was open, so Brown peeped through into the garden within, to the great horror of our companion, who told him if the jealous Turk saw him he would instantly send a bullet into him.

This officer—who, as I believe I have already explained, is a Roman Catholic Christian—took us to his house, and introduced us to his sister, an exceedingly pretty woman. The indoor costume of the Albanian ladies is much more becoming than the ugly scarlet garment that completely conceals their beauty in the streets. This lady was the wife of a wealthy Christian, and her dress was exceedingly costly. The jacket was stiff with beautiful gold embroidery, and large gold coins hung from her neck and girdle.

The manners of an Albanian lady are very pretty and gracious. She brought us coffee with her own hands—small and beautifully-formed as are those of all her race—and sat by us on a heap of cushions, deftly made herself a cigarette, and commenced smoking. She conversed with us in broken Italian, which fell very prettily from her charming lips.

The women of this country do not wither up into old hags by the time they are thirty, as do most orientals and southerners, but preserve their peachy complexions and youthful beauty as long as do the women of our own island. It is true they often get over-corpulent, owing to their exceedingly sedentary lives. A woman of the higher orders but rarely leaves her house; and as she is perpetually squatting cross-kneed, in Turkish fashion, on a divan, or rug, her lower limbs become rather deformed, the result being that her walk is a very ungraceful waddle, rather like that of a well-fed duck.

Our friend's sister had been but recently married. Courtship is curiously managed among the Scutarine Christians. The lover—if he can be so called—never sees his intended till the day of his marriage. A young girl is confined in her father's house for a few years before she arrives at a marriageable age. No men but her nearest relatives ever see her. When her parents consider she is old enough, they let it be known among their friends that they have a marriageable daughter on hand. Probably the young lady's brother will come up to you—if you are a good catch—some day in the street, and say, "You are just the man I wanted to see. My sister is now fourteen years of age. You must marry her." It is an insult to refuse such an offer, for it is generally looked upon as a great honour. However, if the Benedick be rather doubtful as to the advantages of the match, and is desirous of ascertaining whether his proposed bride be endowed with personal attractions, he goes off to an old woman, whose profession it is to intervene in such cases. She calls on the bride, inspects her, and returns to give him an unbiassed summing-up of the young lady's qualities. If he is satisfied, the wedding-day is fixed, but not till the last moment does he view his bride. After the marriage ceremony a very curious performance is gone through. The Albanians entertain peculiar ideas as regards women. To linger with, to be affectionate with, the fair sex, they consider to be degrading to a man's dignity, unfitting him for the sterner business of war. Thus the youth affects to despise the sex, is very shy of showing the slightest regard for it. His sentiments, indeed, are very much those of English boys of a certain age, who would blush to be seen playing with girls. Now, during the marriage feast the bride retires to a room. The bridegroom refuses to follow, and is bound to offer strong resistance; while the other guests—father-in-law, mother-in-law, and all—slap and push in the sham-reluctant one, who at last has to yield to superior numbers, and enters the chamber.

As a young lady is so closely confined to her parents' house until the day of her marriage, she naturally is very anxious to quit a single state, which is by no means a state of blessedness.

Should years go by, and no suitable youth accept her hand—for, as I have shown, he can hardly be said to demand it—one course is open to her, in order that she may gain that freedom she yearns after. She becomes a nun, and adopts the white robe of the Scutarine sisters.

The nuns here are by no means confined within great stone walls, as in some countries. They must attend certain services at the church, but at other times they wander about at their own sweet will, and enjoy an absolute liberty that none others of their sex ever acquire in the East. As a natural consequence, if scandal is to be believed, their lives are not entirely unbrightened with flirtations with the other sex.

CHAPTER X.

The bazaar—Turkish gipsies—The vendetta—An assassin—A way to pay debts—Bosnian refugees—A card-party—Paving-stones—Burglars—Army doctors—Change for a ten pound note—Our horses.

AFTER this we visited the bazaar. Imagine a labyrinth of narrow lanes, paved with large round blocks, polished by the feet of many generations; the open booths laden with every variety of European and Eastern goods; the roofs of every height and at every angle, projecting far over on either side—almost meeting in places—joined by festoons of vines, that keep out the glare of the midday sun; and a thick crowd of armed men and veiled women, some mounted, some on foot, in every variety of barbaric costume.

Here is an armourer's shop, the owner, a sour-looking Mohammedan, in snowy festinelle, jacket stiff with gold embroidery, sits cross-legged on his counter, surrounded with every sort of weapon. The Arnaut gun, with flint lock, narrow steel stock beautifully worked, and Damascened barrel fully five feet long, silver inlaid, and hooped with gilt bands, first attracts our attention. The barrels of these guns are rarely of Albanian make, but have been handed down from father to son for generations, and are re-stocked over and over again ere they are condemned. Most of them are of Venetian make; the marks of the most famous gunmakers of the old republic are found inscribed on them. I came across several Tower-marked barrels of antique date, seeming strange in their Albanian stocks. Here we have yataghans, some with plain ivory hilt, others glittering with gold and precious stones, worth a prince's ransom. Here is the long-barrelled Miridite pistol, with quaintly-carved brass stock. Here all the accessories for killing one's fellows—cartridge belts, carved brass cartridge and oil-rag boxes, flints soaking in a pan of water, and so on.

The next stall is a potter's. He works steadily at his wheel, and surrounds himself with gracefully-formed bowls and pitchers of red clay.

Then we have the fruiterer: pomegranates, figs, oranges, vegetables, and fruits too unknown to us, lie in profusion on his counter.

Here is a worker in leather. He provides you with richly-ornamented saddlery, belts for your sweetheart ornamented with the heads of pins, purses, and the curious treble sack which the Arnaut straps in front of him to hold his yataghan and two lengthy flint pistols. Here is a man embroidering a piece of black or red cloth with the most artistic and delicate patterns in gold or silk. This is to be portion of the garment of a woman of rank.

Here is the carpenter. He is at work on a large square box of deal, coarsely painted with bright colours. This is intended to contain the *trousseau* of the bride, and is the prominent object of the woman's apartment in an Albanian house.

In short you can buy anything in the bazaar, from a horse to a para's worth of halvar.

One of the most curious sights of the bazaar is its gipsy quarter. After traversing one or two sordid alleys, one comes upon a sort of terrace, where, scorning the sun or rain, unprovided with stall or booth, are the zingali tinkers. A wilder and more uncouth lot I never cast eyes upon. Dressed, or rather ragged, in a strange Oriental costume of their own, blackened by exposure, speaking a tongue unknown to all here, there is something very uncanny in them—no wonder that the superstitious Arnaut fears and dislikes them. The women are unveiled, their breasts are bare, and the old hags could well stand as models for a witch of Endor, or any other unearthly and fearsome thing in female human form.

The gipsy has a greater *raison d'être* here than elsewhere in Europe. The proud races of these regions, more especially the Montenegrins, consider it degrading in the highest degree to work in iron, except in the case of the manufacture of arms. Thus, whereas the Albanians of Scutari, Jakova, and Priserin are excellent workers in other metals, all tinkering is left to the despised zingali.

It is quite the proper thing to have a stall in the bazaar. Men of the highest rank sit behind their wares for a few hours of the day, not perhaps caring much whether they sell or not; but this crowded mart is the common rendezvous, and answers the purpose of a club.

As you force your way through the crowd some friend will recognize you, and beckon you to squat by him on his counter, among the cheap Manchester goods, while you talk over the latest gossip over coffee and cigarettes. We soon had formed so many friendships, that a stroll through the bazaar meant for us the swallowing of prodigious quantities of the thick Eastern coffee, which, by the way, is the best of all, if properly made.

It is by no means unusual to have your shopping disturbed by the report of fire-arms. I have already alluded to the blood feud, or vendetta of Albania. This is here carried to an extent quite unknown in other countries. Indeed, the Franciscan missionaries told me that it is very rare indeed to find a really old man in the mountains, the chances being so much in favour of any given man being killed sooner or later in these constant feuds.

It is in the bazaar, on market-days, that men of two families engaged in a vendetta are most likely to meet. You can generally tell whether a man has a feud on hand, by his furtive look; his pistols are cocked, he carries his gun also cocked in his hand, and looks behind him constantly, for fair play is unknown here. To stab a man behind his back is quite legitimate.

The Arnauts are Roman Catholics, and, as Christians, are by law forbidden to carry arms in the towns. But these powerful tribes are too strong to heed the government regulations. No Arnaut ever comes into the town without his arms, and no one dares interfere with him.

Our friend the gendarme took us to the stall of a friend of his—a notable man, Bektsé Tchotché by name. He was an ill-featured Albanian Mussulman, about forty years of age, dressed in a national costume that must have cost hundreds of pounds, so rich it was. The blade of his yataghan was inlaid with an elaborate gold device from point to hilt. Its handle was rough with large diamonds. His long Albanian pistols were gold hilted, and beautifully carved. This fellow, a man of rank, does not seem to carry on any ostensible trade at his stall, but it was hung with a collection of weapons similar to those on his person. Our gendarme whispered to us, "This is a brave man; much respected; has killed more of his fellow-townsmen than any other Scutarine."

Imagine a policeman in England seriously pointing out, as an admirable character and brave nobleman, the most atrocious murderer of the county. Yet this is what this Bektsé Tchotché is. Murder is not a crime here, however cold-blooded and cowardly. The assassin has but to fear the vengeance of the family—there are no police to interfere with him, especially if he be a Mohammedan. This state of things breeds in the towns a race of ferocious bullies, ready and waiting to wash out any fancied affront with your heart's blood. This man, who is in the enjoyment of several hundreds of pounds sterling per annum, has devoted himself entirely to murder. If you meet him in the town you see him sitting erect on a gaily equipped horse, which he encourages to prance and caracole from one side of the street to the other, to the great danger of passers-by. In Albania furious riding is not an offence—in fact, it is difficult to find what is. If an unoffending passer-by jolt against him accidentally on his promenade, a bullet is most probably sent into him *instanter*. As all his pistols are at full cock, and have hair triggers, they not unfrequently go off accidentally in the crowded bazaar.

Perfectly incredible to any one who has not visited these countries, is the light in which assassination is regarded. It is more an amusement than anything else — the sport of men. Walk through the streets of Scutari, and you will find the marks of bullets on every house.

The following was quite a recent affair. A young swell one morning was presented with his account, a few shillings only, by his shoemaker. His noble blood could not suffer the indignity long. He walked down the bazaar, found the beast of a tradesman standing in front of his stall, holding his child in his arms, and, without a word, blew his brains out. This gentleman, I need hardly say, is still at large, and swaggers about as usual.

We drank coffee with Bektsé Tchotché, and had a long conversation with him, the gendarme acting as interpreter. He was very kind and polite, and invited us to see him again.

The bazaar at Scutari is full of strange sights, but the most strange and pitiful is a scene one can witness every day outside a certain baker's, who has made a contract with the government. Here for hours patiently waits a miserable crowd of wretches, men, women, and children, thin and pallid, with— yes, even smelling of—starvation. At last a door opens in the loft, and at once they seem to wake from their death-like lethargy; they press up, each trying to be first; they raise their lean arms, and utter prayers and objurgations, hoarse and cracked with hunger. A piece of undercooked maize bread is given to each, and they depart, devouring it in silence. These are Bosnian refugees, families that have emigrated from their homes at the instance of the Turkish government, which now can do so little for them. Better for them had they stayed in their native valleys, and trusted to the justice of the Austrian giaours. Outside the town, by the roadside, one comes across some that are so worn with travel and hunger that they have not the energy to come with the others to receive the scant rations. Here is a typical group. A veiled woman, sitting patiently by the wayside, with several small children lying by her, all starving, and one evidently dying. The father is dead—killed while resisting the infidels, far away in Bosnia. These unfortunates do not beg—they sit there in mute apathy. The children, maybe, crouch up nearer to their mother when they see a giaour passing. If you show some small coins, and beckon to them, the eldest child will perhaps take courage, and painfully drag itself to you, will take the gift, look wonderingly at you with his big eyes (unnaturally big in the white shrunk face), say not a word, and return to his mother to pour what he has received into her lap. The mother all the time sits there impassive, to all outward appearance, quite heedless of what is going on, and utters not a word. It is the daily sight of these poor wretches, and the tales they have to tell, that so excited the Albanian Mussulmen to resist *à outrance* any occupation of their country by Austria, for of course that power is considered by them as the accursed cause of all this suffering.

We returned to the house of our friend the gendarme, and had a most interesting conversation with him on the customs of his country. He narrated to us, among other things, the last little affair in the way of blood feuds.

"A friend of mine," said he, "was playing at cards in the bazaar with another gentleman. The latter accused my friend of cheating. His reply, of course, was a pistol-bullet, which instantly killed the other. My friend, knowing that many of the dead man's relations were about, escaped from the town to a house he has in the mountains, where he could stay in safety for awhile. The relations of the other, being unable to avenge his death on the person of his murderer, adopted the following very clever plan to entrap and kill, without incurring any risk themselves, the nearest relative of my friend, his father. Two men went to the old man's house, and told him that his son had been slain by a man of Koplik, and that his murderer was now staying in a khan on the road to that village. They offered to accompany him and assist him to avenge his son's death. The old man swallowed the bait without suspicion. On a lonely part of the road, as he rode somewhat in advance of his two companions, they at the same moment fired their pistols into his back, then cutting off his head, sent it in a package to his son."

Thus are things managed in this pleasant land of Albania.

It was dark before we left our friend's house, so he sent his Miridite servant to accompany us with a lantern to our hotel.

Scutari is not lit by night with lamps of any kind, so it is almost impossible to find one's way in the dark through the narrow intricate alleys. Besides, as the paving is laid down carelessly, to say the least of it, one would run a good chance of breaking one's neck, if one dispensed with the services of a link-man. One occasionally comes across deep pits in the middle of a street, or against a rough stone projecting up quite three feet above the average level of the others. As the town is subject to floods, high stepping-stones are placed across the streets at intervals. All this makes walking in the dark exceeding unpleasant in this city.

I said somewhere back that the police have little to do in Scutari. They have one function at any rate. They patrol the streets at night, and arrest all who are not provided with lit lanterns. This rule is strictly enforced. If any one were walking lanternless any night in the town, and did not immediately respond to the patrol's challenge and surrender himself, he would most probably receive a rifle-bullet or so into him. Burglars, provided they carry lamps, are, as far as I can make out, not interfered with by the police. An attempt to break into our consul's house was made not long ago. A watchful *cavasse* (body-servant) saw the men in the garden, and opened fire on them with his gun from a window. The fire was returned, and kept up for half an hour or so between the two parties, simply by way of passing the time pleasantly, I suppose. The Albanians are vile shots, and no damage was done on either side, beyond may be a window or so broken. The police kept carefully out of the way all the time.

Three army doctors dined with us at the hotel table d'hôte. They were not in a happy state of mind. Their whole conversation was a vehement abuse of the Turkish Government. As they understood Italian we were able to join in the talk. One of them, a very amusing old fellow, an Armenian, waxed very warm over his grievances. "Ah, Signor, you have no idea what a corrupt, vile thing this Turkish Government is. The court eats all the country. We who work, the employés of the state, the doctors, the soldiers, never receive any pay now. We are put off with excuses on excuses, lies on lies. As long as they think they can obtain our labour for nothing, not a para will they let slip through their fingers. Look at my case. I have been a doctor in the Turkish army for forty years, I have been through the Crimea, over all Asia, in the service of the Porte. I am entitled to a good pension. I have been day after day to the office at Constantinople, and put my case before the authorities. They put me off with all sorts of fair promises, but I knew what that meant, so went to them day after day, and worried them so much that they decided to get rid of me in some way. 'There is a permanent hospital in Scutari, in Albania,' they told me. 'In consideration of your long service we appoint you as head doctor of it. Start at once to your post.' Now that I have travelled all this way, at my own expense mind you, what do I find? The permanent hospital no longer exists—it is a myth, and they knew it at Constantinople all the time, and no doubt chuckled merrily, when I had turned my back, at the clever way they had rid themselves of the importunate old nuisance."

Our friend the gendarme called on us after dinner. He too had his grievance. He had just called on his commandant, in hopes of receiving some small portion of the arrears of pay due to him. The following brief conversation ensued:—

"What do you want here, Lieutenant P.?"

"I want money."

"What? Eh! Money! What on earth for?"

"To procure bread."

"Ah! bread; that is well. Do you know what there is in the *caisse?*"

"No."

"Well, there is nothing; and I see little chance of there being a single para there for some time. So go, young man, and do not indulge in extravagant habits. I advise you as an older man."

After a few consultations with Mr. Green, Brown and myself determined to carry out our original plan of riding to Janina, and of visiting Priserin on our way, if the Leaguesmen were willing to receive us in that city.

Our friend the gendarme offered to accompany us the whole way for a small consideration. This suited us exactly. For with him we could converse, and the chances were small of our meeting people who could understand any Western language, on our route. Besides, the Turkish government compels all travellers to take an escort of zaptiehs. At certain stages these are changed, and another escort is given, of greater or less numerical strength according to the state of the country to be traversed. In the company of this officer, we should probably be able to dispense with this nuisance, except perhaps on a few stages where brigands were supposed to be prowling about. An escort of zaptiehs is really of little use; for when brigands are come across here, it is not in twos and threes, but in overwhelming numbers.

We were rather surprised when our intended companion told us that he could easily procure letters of safe-conduct for us to the chiefs of the League at Priserin and Jakova, as he himself had many intimate friends among the head men of that formidable organization, at Scutari. Curiously illustrative was this of the present condition of this country. Here was an official of the Turkish Government, an officer of police, openly associating and sympathizing with rebels, whose avowed object it is to throw off the Turkish yoke by force of arms, and place a prince of their own choice on the old stone throne of Scanderbeg at Kroia.

The next thing to do was to make preparations for our journey. We had spent all our gold, so found that we were obliged to change some of our English notes. This was no easy matter. After some difficulty, with the assistance of Mr. Green we found an old Christian merchant, Shouma by name, reputedly of great wealth. He might be able to manage the little affair for us.

L

We called on him, and according to the custom of the country we indulged in coffee, sweetmeats, sherbet, and cigarettes before commencing to state our business. Very suspiciously he looked at the notes. Bills of exchange he would have discounted without hesitation; I believe our own promissory notes would have satisfied him. But in governments this wise man had no faith. He did not believe in a paper currency.

He had observed how in his own country it had depreciated till at last it was absolutely valueless. He knew that even Austria's notes were worth considerably less than the sum they are supposed to represent. I tried to explain to him what Bank of England notes really were—what the difference between a convertible and an inconvertible paper currency was; but Shouma evidently considered that the convertible paper was a still more subtle device of a more clever government to hoodwink and swindle the people.

However, he agreed to change a ten pound note for us, provided that Mr. Green guaranteed that it really was worth ten golden sovereigns. Mr. Green was of course willing to do this for us. Shouma accordingly took our note, but told us that it would take three days at least to rake together so large a sum as ten pounds in Scutari. He would go that very day to the bazaar, and get as much as he could, for us to go on with.

Change for a Ten Pound Note. 147

In three days, a huge packet of metallic discs, of every size and inscription, was ready for us. This was accompanied by a document, lengthy as the manifest of a mail steamer, specifying the value of this wonderful ten pounds' worth of coins.

He gave us 131 piastres and a fraction for each sovereign. It took us two hours to count and verify our change. There were silver medjidiés at $22\frac{1}{2}$ piastres each, all sorts of curious concave plates of base metal, worth $11\frac{1}{2}$, $6\frac{3}{4}$, $13\frac{1}{2}$, and many other odd sums nasty to calculate.

There were Greek coins, Russian roubles, old Austrian swanzickers bearing the effigies of Maria Theresa, Peruvian and Mexican dollars, and I know not what besides. Verifying one's change, is no joke in Albania.

To shop in the bazaar of Scutari is a maddening operation, unless one heroically resigns oneself to the certainty of being cheated twice over in every transaction; for not only must one bargain fiercely and cunningly, and beat down the price the merchant asks for an article in the first instance, but after one has come to terms, and is about to hand over his fifty piastres, say, another still warmer and more utterly confusing discussion is sure to ensue as to the value of the coins one presents to him.

The piece of money you yourself received as a twenty-piastre bit, he insists is worth only eighteen.

"See here," he says, "this swanzicker you give me has a hole through it; that diminishes its value by two paras." Two or three neighbours are called in to decide the question. Each has a diffcrent opinion on the subject.

The fact is that all money is acceptable here, and that, especially since Turkey's reduced circumstances, the currency consists of the old, semi-defaced coinage of a dozen nations at least, whose value is arrived at by guesswork. I met no one in Albania capable of telling off-hand how many piastres a given piece was worth.

We spent the three days Shouma had given us, in preparing for our journey, and seeing as much as we could of the habits and customs of the Scutarines.

As we had made up our minds to ride, we paid a visit to the bazaar to purchase two horses. All sorts of extraordinary animals were produced, and refused.

At last we came across one that struck our fancy—a long-legged, extremely lean creature, tall for the country, of a red-brick colour.

Brown, who is a horsey man, proceeded to examine him in a scientific manner, to the admiration of the Arnaut stablemen.

He pointed out the weak points of the animal by signs to the dealer, who was quite as sharp as any of his fraternity in England.

Brown, wishing to express his disapproval of the extremely emaciated condition of the horse, pointed to his ribs; whereon the man, misunderstanding his meaning, deliberately counted them before him—a very easy process in the case of this Albanian Rosinante—and indignantly signified to my companion that he was too much of a gentleman to offer for sale a horse that was not provided with a sufficient number of those necessary costal supporters.

The animal was then trotted out, down one of the crowded alleys of the bazaar. He found favour in Brown's critical eye, so the bargaining commenced.

"*Sa paré?*" (how much) I asked.

The dealer held up both his hands, and said, "napoleon Frank"—to signify that he wanted ten napoleons.

Brown expressed infinite disgust, and held up two fingers.

The dealer in his turn turned his back, with indignant gesticulations and exclamations at the ridiculously low offer.

At last a bargain was struck, the money counted out, and the purchase delivered to us.

We were mounted at the time on two horses Mr. Green had kindly lent us; so we led off Rosso —as we named our animal, in consequence of his rosy hue—with a rope behind us.

Through Mr. Green we managed to procure another steed, a younger animal, and of more robust habit than the lean and haggard Rosso. From his more gentlemanly appearance we gave him the name of Effendi.

We managed to pick up two saddles in the bazaar—one the regular Turkish saddle, at first so uncomfortable to the novice, but gaudy with flimsy metal ornament; the other was a second-hand Turkish officer's saddle, similar to that used in Europe, and provided with formidable-looking holsters.

We felt very proud of our purchases, and took a long ride the same afternoon over the plain, to a very fine old Venetian bridge that spans a branch of the Bojano, Mr. Green's son accompanying us.

Rosso and Effendi proved to be all that could be desired.

CHAPTER XI.

Our Lady of Scutari—A miracle—The fête—A funeral—A drunken Arnaut—Our escort—Two more Britons—Warm discussion—War—Marco.

THE morrow (October 18th) was the great holiday of North Albania, the day of Our Lady of Scutari.

Long ago all this country was Christian. In this city there then stood a beautiful wooden image of the Virgin Mary. Thousands of the faithful were wont to flock hither year by year to offer their devotions at her feet, and to be healed of their infirmities; for no sick man that had faith was ever known to kiss the white feet of the image and not depart whole.

But it came to pass that a certain priest made himself very unpopular among the people. I do not quite know for what cause, but at any rate a large multitude came to the church one day, and declared that unless something that they desired was granted to them they would then and there abjure the religion of Christ and embrace

Mohammedanism. Rightly or wrongly, the priest would not give in; whereupon the people tore their rosaries from their necks, and marched off to the nearest Mohammedan village, that the mollahs might receive the renegades into the fold of the Prophet; whereupon Our Lady of Scutari, sorrowful and angry at the desertion of those for whom she had wrought so many good things for so many years, left her shrine in this ungrateful land.

That night the wooden image disappeared. It was not heard of for months—when tidings came that on the very same night that this event happened, an image of the Virgin miraculously entered a church in a remote village of Italy, and there took up its abode. A loud voice was also heard, crying out over Scutari, that not till the last Turki (Mohammedan) had left Albania would Our Lady of Scodra be appeased and forgive her children: then, and not till then, would she return to her old shrine.

This day was the anniversary of the miraculous departure of the image, long ago; and an impressive service was held in the great ugly square church of the Christians in this city.

The interior of this building is almost entirely devoid of any ornament whatever, and bears no resemblance to any church elsewhere.

The priests that minister to the spiritual wants of the Albanians are Franciscans and Jesuits, all of whom are Italians. The Franciscan monks have a convent and schools. The Jesuits have tried their best to monopolize the education of the people, but are not much liked.

It was difficult, standing in this bleak building, in the midst of so wild and outlandish though very devout a congregation, to imagine oneself attending a Christian service.

The fierce-eyed shaven-headed Arnaut mountaineer jostled with the mild-looking Scutarine Christian and kilted Mussulman; for those of the other faith, curiously enough, offer their devotions on this day to the mother of the Christ whom they despise. Indeed though one half the Albanians call themselves Christians, and the other half profess to be Mohammedans, there is really little distinction between them. The Mohammedans worship the Virgin Mary; the Christians make pilgrimages to the sepulchres of Mussulman saints, and mingle all sorts of grotesque alien superstitions with their Christianity, which the priesthood in vain strive to eradicate.

I was told that even some relics of the old Greek paganism linger in these mountains.

I myself have seen the Arnauts attempt to read the future from the entrails of a sheep which they had slain for a feast.

Before the service we had an opportunity of witnessing a Christian funeral. The coffin was borne on the shoulders of men, while the women followed at a distance, crying and wailing, as is and has been the custom, in all the East, for all time:—

"He was strong in the chase, he was handsome, he was lovable, he was brave. Alas! no more will he be loved, no more will his swift feet carry him to the hunt. His enemies will rejoice, and throw away their fear. Alas! alas! he has gone from us! he will be hidden in the cold earth."

In the evening a band played outside the church, and the jolly Franciscan monks tucked up their gowns, and proceeded to amuse the crowd with several balloons, which they filled with hot air and liberated, to the great delight of all.

It was a good-humoured though savage-looking mob, and would set a good example to many a gathering of Western civilization. The streets were gaily lit with many-coloured Chinese lanterns. As we walked home after the termination of the proceedings, I noticed that there were one or two cases of drunkenness.

There was one man, an Arnaut, pretty far gone. As I consider the different effects of alcohol on the brains of different races to be a very interesting and curious study, I stood and watched the mountaineer for some time, at a safe distance; for he bristled with arms of course; and if a drunken man, carrying with him two loaded pistols, a gun, and yataghan, should run amuck, or conceive a sudden dislike to the English foreigners, the consequences might be unpleasant. However, he did nothing of the kind. The sole effect of the raki was to make him exceedingly devotional. He knelt down, raised his hands, and prayed in a loud voice, and with a most intense and passionate earnestness. He swung backwards and forwards—wrung his hands, as he worked himself into a phrenzy of religious excitement. Then he kissed the .muddy ground over and over again with fervour, under the impression perhaps that he was still at the foot of the empty shrine of the Madonna.

Lastly, he fell prone, face down in the mud, dead drunk, when his friends raised him and carried him off, with looks of shame on their faces, for drunkenness is considered to be a beastly and degrading vice in this uncivilized country.

While we were breakfasting on the following morning, our friend the gendarme appeared, with a very downcast and despondent visage.

"The beasts!" he said. "O, these Turks! I cannot go with you, friends. I had obtained leave, as you know, to accompany you on your journey through Albania. Well, late last night I was sent for, and told that I must stay at Scutari. They had seen me often in your company, and, as is their custom, became jealous and suspicious; so they have got up some idle excuse to prevent my going with you. This is the way they treat us. They give us no pay; and when we do get a chance of making a little money, do their best to get in our way."

Our poor friend was very cut up, and naturally so, for to be guard of a party of Inglezi was a rare windfall for him, and very acceptable in these hard times.

The authorities sent us a passport, and a very strange-looking being, who was to be our escort on the morrow, one man being deemed a sufficient protection, for the first stage at any rate. He was a tall, miserable-looking zaptieh, in very ragged uniform. His face was of extraordinary length, and lantern-jawed. He was almost skeleton-like in his extreme thinness. He had evidently not known what a good meal meant for a very long time.

We discovered him to be an intensely stupid and unintelligent being. This did not promise well. Here we were, two Englishmen, utterly ignorant of Turkish or Albanian, about to ride right across the country in the company of a man who would not be of the slightest use to us in any way.

We gave him a good feed, in hopes that this might develope some traces of intelligence in his dense skull. All in vain. The only effect was, that after having thoroughly gorged himself, he closed his eyes, gave vent to a sort of choking sound, and fell fast asleep.

Everything was ready; we had bid adieu to our Scutarine friends, left orders that our horses should be brought round early on the morrow—then we retired to our beds among the sausages.

It was scarce dawn. There was a loud knock at our door—a rather violent knock. The door opened; we expected to see the smiling face of Toshli, who had come to announce the arrival of our ghostly zaptieh and our brave steeds; but to our astonishment there entered, boisterously, two bronzed and travel-stained Britons—in short, the long-lost Jones and Robinson, whom we had given up long ago.

They stood laughing before us; but Brown and myself considered it incumbent upon us to receive them in a slightly distant and dignified manner as we sat up in our beds. We asked them to give an explanation of their great dilatoriness in catching us up.

We found that they had started from England a fortnight after us, but had been delayed at Cattaro and other ports, in consequence of some extremely ingenious arrangement Robinson, the inventor, had made for receiving money at different places on the route.

They had followed in our footsteps exactly—had taken boat from Trieste to Cattaro, and thence walked, viâ Cettinje, to Rieka, where they had taken a londra for Scutari. We inquired where the white elephant and other Robinsoniana were.

They had left them at Cettinje, they said, and were going to return for them. This further delay was by no means pleasing to Brown and myself. We laid our programme before them, and expected that they would fall in with it at once. A very warm discussion ensued, very nearly resulting in a re-separation of our forces.

They had been very well received, it seems, by the Montenegrins, and had promised some of the chieftains at Cettinje that they would return to that capital as soon as they had seen Scutari.

The war between the principality and the Albanians, so long talked of, was, they said, now but a question of a few days. They had been invited to accompany the army of Prince Nikita, which was on the point of advancing on Gussinje, as the honoured guests of the general in command.

There are certainly two sides to every question. From the little we had seen of the two countries, Brown and myself had formed a decided preference for the Albanians over the Montenegrins; but we found that our two friends were full of praises of the Black Mountaineers, and abuse of the Skipitars. The Montenegrins have rather a knack of wheedling over strangers to their own views of the question. Jones and Robinson, however, to a great extent modified their opinions later on, when we had seen a little more of both sides.

The discussion progressed with considerable warmth. Our recently found friends insisted on returning to Montenegro. Brown and myself were very loth to give up our projected ride across the little-known countries of North Albania. We often wandered from the point into hot dispute as to the virtues or the reverse of the respective races. Ultimately a compromise was effected. We decided to convert Rosso and Effendi into baggage animals, and walk from Scutari to Podgoritza, an important town, acquired by Montenegro from Turkey during the late war, and which was but two days' march from Gussinje. Here the Montenegrin forces were to concentrate, before advancing against the enemy. If we found that war was really intended, we agreed to carry out the programme of our friends. If we found that it was being indefinitely delayed, we would return to Scutari, and march to Previso by the route Brown and myself had decided on.

Brown and myself gave in with great reluctance, feeling that our friends, after delaying us so long, were now about to take us on a wild goose chase after a phantom war. I do not think either of us recovered that sweetness of temper which distinguishes us until after the dinner we partook of that evening at the hospitable board of the British Consulate.

During the above discussion our ghostly zaptieh was announced. With the aid of our landlord we tried to explain to him that his services were no longer needed by us. This man, as I have said, was the incarnation of stupidity; as a Turkish soldier, he was also a model of obedience to those who were put in authority over him.

He had been ordered to conduct us to Priserin—so much had got into his head; and conduct us to Priserin he would, notwithstanding our insistence that we had now altered our intentions. "The Pasha told me to take you to Priserin," was all we could get out of him. He would have attempted to take us there by force, I believe, had we not quieted him with another full meal, which had the same soporific effect as that of the previous day.

When we told Mr. Green of our altered plans, in the evening, he remarked that at any rate our throats would be safe in Montenegro, which is more than they would be in this country. "But," he added, "if you visit Podgoritza you will not be able to return here and visit Priserin. They will have heard of your friendship with the Montenegrin general, and will inevitably take you as spies, and treat you as such in a very summary manner. If you return here and wish to travel to Janina, you must do so by the other route, which takes you through the cities of Tirana, Elbessan, and Berat.

The next day we made preparations for our journey.

As it was a doubtful question whether we should find food on the road to Podgoritza, an unfrequented track, with rather a bad reputation for Arnauts, we purchased a horse-hair saddle-bag, and laid up a good stock of rice bread, mutton, raki, and other necessaries. Robinson had brought his cooking apparatus with him to Scutari, and was very anxious to bring it into use on the earliest occasion.

The evening before our start we very luckily came across a man who had served as groom to Captain Sale, of the late frontier commission. He seemed to understand a word or two of English and Italian, and had a very good character from the Consulate. So we hired him for a month. A very useful fellow he turned out to be. He was dressed in full Arnaut costume, which never left his back during the whole of his stay with us—five weeks, and yet, in some mysterious manner, it ever appeared snowy and new, indeed, his appearance did us credit. He was a young fellow of pleasing countenance, the chief characteristic of which was a perpetual grin.

M

Like all I met of his race, he was faithful and honest, and soon became attached to his masters. His preparations for the journey did not require much time, for his luggage consisted simply of a large gingham umbrella.

CHAPTER XII.

March to Podgoritza—An Albanian khan—Our cook—The Fund—Across the lake—Night visitors—The frontier—Podgoritza—The armourer—The war minister—Dobra Pushka.

OVER our last glass of grog before turning in for the night, we had determined to start at daybreak this morning. So abominable was the weather, however, that we preferred to indulge in the comfort of our beds a little longer. An unbroken mass of cloud covered the whole sky, from which poured down a steady deluge, which had a deliberate look about it, as if it had no intention of ceasing for a month at least. Jones looked out of the window, scanned the horizon mournfully, and remarking that he thought the rainy season would soon begin, got into bed again.

At last we mustered courage enough to rise, ordered a substantial breakfast, and sent the faithful Marco to saddle Rosso and Effendi. When Rosso was brought in front of the hotel, he evidently objected to standing out there in the rain while we breakfasted in comfort within; so he walked into the room in which we sat, and made a very fair meal off a deal box that stood in the corner. Our saddle-bags and blankets were placed on the horses' backs, and the expedition started. Our gendarme and landlord saw us well out of the town, where a stirrup-cup was indulged in. We must have looked very imposing: first Marco in his Arnaut dress, sheltering himself with a huge umbrella, the only article of luggage he brought with him; then the two horses; and lastly, our four selves.

All in top-boots—Jones, Brown, and myself well protected with hooded military macintoshes we had bought in Turkey, while Robinson was enveloped in a ponderous English yeomanry greatcoat, which must have weighed something when it was thoroughly soaked. Our rifles were slung to our shoulders. Jones was the proud bearer of an Arnaut gun, of which I shall have to say more anon. He also carried a pocket filter, slung to his shoulders.

This day's journey was certainly not a pleasnt one. The road from Scutari to Podgoritza is not much of a road at the best of times; it is a mere track. For the first day's march it traverses the plain which borders the east shore of the lake.

This day it was difficult to know what was intended for lake, what for road; it was all the same. The lake had the advantage, if anything, of being the less muddy of the two. We were up to our knees in water all day. I endeavoured to enter into conversation with Marco, and was grieved to find he was a fraud. Yesterday, when we hired him, I spoke to him in Italian and French, curiously mixed together; for I was told he understood a little of both these languages. To everything I said he replied briskly, *Ça bonne, monsor, ça bonne.* This is the man for us, I said; he understands all I say. "Then he must, indeed, be a wonderful man," my friends replied; "let us have him."

But alas! I now discovered that Marco's linguistic powers were very limited. Give him an order; he never confessed to his absolute ignorance of what you were talking about, but blithely came out with his perpetual *ça bonne, ça bonne,* as if that was all that was required of him. However, by degrees I discovered what words he knew of French, what of Italian, and what of English (for he had even picked up some words of our tongue when in the service of the commissioners). With the addition of a few words of Sclav and Albanian, I then manufactured a mongrel tongue, which was common to Marco and myself, and utter gibberish to any one else. About midday we halted for lunch. We stood up to our knees in mud and water under the pouring rain, ate sausage, and each in turn made use of the filter, which was placed in the muddy water of the road, while the purified fluid was sucked through an indiarubber tube.

Marco was much astonished and pleased at this proceeding. A tot of rum all round completed our modest repast. On the way we were joined by a man who was also travelling to Podgoritza— a Montenegrin, on horseback. Being alone, he was glad to join our party, well armed as we were, for the Arnauts that inhabit the mountains that were to the right of us have a bad name, and are much given to plundering travellers.

At last a large house rose before us. "That is the khan of Coplik," said Marco. "We must pass the night here, for the next house of any kind is eight hours off."

We entered the khan, and found it to be a more luxurious place than we expected to find. An upper room was given to us for our use. It had no windows, but the rough stone wall and raftered roof admitted plenty of daylight, not to mention rain and wind. The floor was also well ventilated, as was the door that opened on the wooden gallery outside. As Jones remarked, our chamber combined the comforts of a home with the sanitary advantages of a hydropathic establishment. There was no furniture of any kind, and the whole of the elegant chamber was blackened with smoke. We soon spread our blankets, and made ourselves very comfortable. We had brought some provisions with us, but Marco was sent out in search of any dainty there might be in the establishment. In a Turkish khan you are supplied with shelter and firing; bedding and provisions you are supposed to bring with you.

The landlord, a grim-looking Arnaut, came in with Marco, and said he could let us have two fowls, but would be pleased if we came out and shot them. He evidently wished to see our weapons in use, so we gratified him. Our Nimrod, Robinson, blew one rooster to pieces. Brown was satisfied with knocking off the head of the other with a Winchester bullet. (We were charged 5d. each for them.) A brazier of charcoal was brought up to our room, and a large pot; whereupon Brown, taking upon himself the office of cook, commenced to prepare our meal, and very successful he was.

He cut up the fowls, and boiled them up with slices of sausage, macaroni, grease-meal, salt, pepper, all from our commissariat bag. I am not sure he did not even add some of the flea powder as seasoning. We watched him hungrily and anxiously. Awful would have been his end had he spoiled that dish. Wet through as we were, we thoroughly enjoyed the meal, which we washed down with the rum we had brought with us, and raki we bought from the khanji. Very contented and jovial I know we all felt afterwards as we squatted round the fire on our blankets, smoking our pipes and drinking our coffee. Marco too seemed to thoroughly appreciate our cookery, and grinned happily for the rest of the day.

Our retiring for the night did not involve much preparation. To take off one's boots and roll oneself up in one's blanket sufficed. Robinson suggested that the door should be left open, as the fumes of the charcoal fire might suffocate us in the night. Considering the number and size of the orifices in roof and wall we thought this would be excess of caution. The prudent Robinson had also heard many awful tales of Eastern khans, and suggested that some one should remain awake. In England, before starting on this expedition, we had determined to station regular watches every night. Here was a good opportunity to begin, but somehow no one seemed quite to see it; I think we were too sleepy. One good and useful suggestion was, however, made. This was, that when sleeping in perilous places we should keep Brown away from his flea-powder. He would then of a certainty keep an admirable watch. In the middle of the night a gruff and sleepy voice was heard to issue from the blanket in which Jones was enveloped,

"Bother that crumb." "What is the matter?" we inquired. "There is a crumb in my bed," was the reply. "It got under my side, and woke me up." On searching for the crumb, Jones found it was his Colt revolver that had thus troubled his sleep. We slept very well in spite of rain, wind, and insects, and were up at daybreak, packing our baggage for the day's march.

As we gradually discovered each other's talents, we apportioned to each his particular duty on the march or in the camp. Brown had displayed such great culinary skill that we unanimously elected him *chef* to the expedition. As a branch of this important office, it was his province to decide what vegetables and other comestibles should be purchased when the commissariat bag was light. He was also a capital muleteer, and would urge on our steeds, when lazily inclined, with considerable results. Robinson was so occupied with the carriage of his weighty rifle, that none of his talents had scope for manifestation on the march. However, he was a wonderful man at packing the tent and baggage, and so made himself very useful every morning in getting things in order. Jones, the philosopher, was general supervisor of the others, saw that all went well, and pensively looked on while others worked. On me was inflicted the most arduous duty of all. I was dubbed the

Fund—that is, I was banker and paymaster. This office was conferred on me in consideration of a certain smattering I had of the Latin tongues. French and Italian are far more useful in Turkey than are any other European languages. When we came across the Franciscan missionaries, in the mountains, I conversed with these fluently and rapidly, in dog Latin crossed with Italian—a language that would have much astonished my masters at Westminster in the olden time.

There was one advantage in being Fund. Having command of the wealth of the party, I was followed, flattered, and made much of by the others. Later on, on our return journey across Europe, the office changed hands. Brown became Fund, and the old Fund was neglected and forgotten for the new—such are men.

This was a hard day's march. Our route for many hours lay across the same little cultivated and monotonous plain. We saw but little game, and that we could not get at. We caught glimpses occasionally of the long line of the lake of Scutari, to the left of us; while on our right, behind the rolling plains, rose the huge bare mountains of Castrati. At last, as we approached the termination of the lake, the flat country came to an end, and the mountains fell down to the edge of the water. Our road now became exceedingly difficult, a mere goat-track up and down the rugged hill side, now across *couloirs* of *débris*, as they call them in the Alps, now through jungles of thorn, and now up almost perpendicular rocks. The rain had ceased, and the sun was uncomfortably hot for such work as this. Our Montenegrin fellow-traveller, who started with us this morning, dismounted from his horse, and was obliged to push him bodily over the worst parts. We had to keep a sharp eye on Rosso and Effendi; they slipped and stumbled incessantly. Rosso proved to be the best mountaineer of the two. Effendi was far less sure-footed. This little animal again was so well fed that his circumference was a mathematical circle in form. Thus, as he had none of the Rosinante-like angles of Rosso, which gave hold to the strappings, his pack was continually twisting round and rolling under him. At last, hot and thirsty, we reached a little plateau just over the lake, where were pitched three or four tents, the quarters of a small party of the most utterly miserable-looking Turkish soldiers I had ever cast eyes upon. All were in rags. Their uniforms were supplemented with some garments of the country. They were bare-footed, or wore the native punkoa.

"What important garrison town may this be, Marco?" said Jones.

"*Ça bonne, monsor, ça bonne,*" replied our grinning domestic. I don't know whether the place has a name; I should say it had, being in this country, where three houses constitute a town. There were three officers here, who shared one miserable tent. The poor fellows had not seen pay for a very long time. One, a Crimean medallist, a defender of Kars, was down with fever badly. They invited us into their wretched quarters, and ordered coffee for us. They had no sugar, but this we were able to provide them with. We also had some cakes of chocolate, which we presented to them, and which they seemed very glad to get. They were fine-looking fellows, but all had that sad look which true Turks wear in these latter days. With the aid of Marco as interpreter, we were able to converse with them on various subjects. They seemed to despair of their country, and, like all I met, put all the blame on the evil system of government. They told us that a londra would be here soon, bearing provisions from the fortress of Helm for this post. The londra would then return, and we could go with it, thus saving ourselves a five hours' very rough march. We gladly availed ourselves of the offer, and waited for the arrival of the boat. We studied our maps, and tried to make out where we were, and what branch of the lake this might be which we were to traverse. The maps on this occasion, as on all others, gave no information on the subject. The fact of the matter is, there is no map of this part of the Turkish dominions. The rivers, lakes, and towns, are put in by guess-work.

The londra at last arrived. It was manned by six or seven disreputable and hungry-looking soldiers. The provisions were landed; these consisted of a few maize loaves and a small bag of rice.

We bid adieu to our friends the officers, with a little difficulty persuaded Rosso and Effendi to embark, and were soon gliding swiftly across the smooth lake. In about an hour we had reached the opposite side. Here were three or four houses, occupied by Turkish officers, while the men were camped out on the edge of the lake in tents, so ragged and torn that they must have been next to useless. In the background, a few miles from the lake, there was a steep mountain, on whose summit was a large fortress. This place we found is called Helm. We landed, and at once resumed our march, which lay under the mountain, and across a broad and lengthy plain which lies between Podgoritza and the lake. There was no sign of cultivation anywhere. The plain was a pebbly desert, scanty grass and a sort of prickly thorn being the sole vegetation.

The heavy rain had once more set in, and before we had marched very far, the waters, rushing down from the distant mountains, converted the plain into a lake, across which we waded, the muddy compound rising above our top-boots. Darkness at length came on, so as we should certainly have lost ourselves had we gone much further, we entered a khan, which turned up before us just in time. It was a rougher and less civilized khan than that of the previous evening. There was but one room in it; the floor was of clay; the walls, as usual, black with the smoke of ages; and the ventilation almost too perfect.

They had some goat's flesh here, so we were enabled to make an excellent meal. Being tired after our long march, we then retired to our beds.

Just by the bar, as we chose to call the corner of the room where the raki and wine were stored, there was a broad wooden slab against the wall, supported on logs, and sloping down outward at a slight angle.

This was to serve as our bed for the night. We lay side by side rolled up in our blankets. The neighbourhood was soon made aware of our arrival; the khan was filled with armed Arnauts, who came and stared at us inquisitively, while they whispered to each other in a mysterious manner.

There was something very comic in the situation. There we lay, stretched out in a row on that deal board, for all the world like the corpses lying side by side, in similar fashion, on the marble slab of the Paris morgue.

However, enveloped as we were in our voluminous blankets, nothing could be seen of us but four projecting nasal organs. But this was quite enough for our friends. Throughout the night they came and went through the open door: there were never less than a dozen admiring us at a time.

Towards the morning the bard of the district came in, tuned up his guzla, and favoured us with a dismal selection from his *repertoire*.

His voice was high and cracked, but he sang fiercely and energetically, while all the natives listened, spellbound and silent. I presume he was singing our praises—he was evidently chanting the doings of some great warriors.

Jones at last sneezed so violently in the middle of his song that the minstrel was quite disconcerted, and sadly laying down his instrument, stretched himself on the floor and slept. Being now at peace, we followed his example.

I might as well mention the fact that I have never seen a Montenegrin or Albanian take off his clothes before retiring for the night. I believe, except when one of these people buys a new suit, he never does, on any occasion whatever, undress. The poorer people, who never do indulge in new suits, merely patch up the old while on them.

The next morning, at daybreak, we swallowed some boiling coffee, and prepared for the march. Our toilet was simple enough: as Jones said, "All I have to do is to rub in dubbin on my boots, and sling on my pocket filter, and I am ready."

It was a bright, sunny morning. This change of the weather was very welcome to us, wet through as we had been, night and day, since we left Scutari. Half-way between Helm and Podgoritza a river crosses the plain. The rapid water has eaten for itself a deep, narrow channel with perpendicular sides. This forms the frontier between Turkey and Montenegro. We crossed this torrent on a well-made bridge, in whose centre was a stone, on one side of which were inscribed the arms of the mountain principality, on the other side the star and crescent of the Sublime Porte. From here we saw, far away over the plain, the minarets of Podgoritza, standing out white against a background of dark Montenegrin mountains.

It was not long before we were outside the town. It had been a dreary morning's march. The plain, which with care might return much to the agriculturist, was left bare and uncultivated. One need not search far for a reason. We were on the frontier, on the scene of perpetual border frays. He who sowed here would sow for the whirlwind only.

Close to the town was a rough sentry-box; out stepped a Montenegrin sentry, quite a boy, and challenged us. We amused him by showing him our passports, which he gravely considered, first upside down, then sideways; then he held one up to the sun, then shook his head and returned

them. He questioned Marco as to what we were. "These are consuls Inglesi," replied the faithful one; "English consuls on the spree." This was sufficient. We were saluted and allowed to pass.

I believe that throughout our stay in Montenegro we were invariably taken for English Consuls, on a sort of happy-go-lucky holiday; anyhow, we were highly appreciated by all the natives we came across.

It was very amusing to hear Marco explain us to inquisitive people. Some passers-by would stalk by us—too polite and proud to stare or show any surprise at our appearance; but having passed us, they would stop Marco, and whisper to him, "What are these men?" "Great diplomatists," would reply Marco, with dignity. "Consuls Inglesi. That one in the spectacles is the head diplomatist. All great diplomatists wear spectacles, you know."

We passed through the ruined walls which surround Podgoritza, and marched down several badly-paved streets to the chief khan of the place.

Podgoritza is a considerable town, with a population, I should say, of 8000 at least. It is picturesquely situated on the east bank of the Moracha, a turbulent stream, and one of the chief feeders of the Lake of Scutari. A large proportion of the inhabitants are Mohammedans.

The treaty of Berlin handed over this important Albanian fortress to Montenegro. The Black

Mountaineers had only occupied the place a short time before our arrival. But all seemed to be going on peaceably; the inhabitants appeared quite reconciled to their new government.

Our khan had been recently the house of a wealthy Mohammedan, and was quite an imposing building. An archway led through to a courtyard, surrounded by stables; above the stables ran a wooden gallery, on to which opened the various apartments. It was exactly like some of the old-fashioned inns of the posting days, which one still comes across so frequently in Normandy.

We had a very pleasant chamber handed over to us for our use. A window filled one side of it. As this window was unglazed, this was rather a chilly residence at this time of the year, when the bora blew strong and fresh from the snow-capped mountains. In our honour, one half of the window was glazed. I suppose this exhausted all the glass in the town, for no effort was made to complete the work, though we were here for several days. A divan ran round the wall, on which we were to sleep. They cooked for us at this hotel, but there was little variety in the cuisine; one day stewed fowl and stewed mutton, the next stewed mutton and stewed fowl, and so on. We found there were some bottles of Cyprus wine downstairs, at the bar. We very soon exhausted these, for Cyprus wine seemed a great delicacy, after the rough Albanian wines and rakis.

After breakfast Robinson and Marco rode off to Cettinje, fifteen hours from here, to fetch the tent and the rest of their baggage.

While they were away we explored the town, and made the acquaintance of a very good fellow, Gospodina Milosh, the government armourer, who was now very occupied in putting into order the rifles which the mountaineers brought down to him, anticipating the invasion of Albaniar territory, the orders to march being daily expected. This gentleman had been sent to Vienna to learn his trade, and spoke German well, so was a useful interpreter for us during our stay.

There was a large building adjoining our hotel, which was occupied by the minister of war for Montenegro. It was he who led the highlanders in those successful battles they fought with the Turks on the Herzegovinan frontier during the last war. His name I have forgotten. Every morning we saw him and a dozen chiefs, and others, stalk up and down the river side in front of our window, for it was out of doors he transacted his business, received his despatches, gave his orders, and formed plans for the investment of Gussinje.

The next morning we went outside the town with our landlord (who by the way was a sergeant in the army, as the metal eagle in his cap betokened), for a little practice with our rifles.

We easily beat the natives on this as on all

other occasions, and gave them a very high idea of our skill as rifle shots.

I hit the target (a pocket handkerchief) at a 200 yards' range, at the first shot, which so pleased the spectators that they gave me the name of the "dobra Pushka."

There is a little bazaar in Podgoritza, through which we strolled. We purchased some of the native caps, for it is always advisable to wear these when in Montenegro; the people like one to assume their national head-covering, and have a strong dislike for European hats.

We tried to catch some fish in the river, but failed, so returned to our caravanserai for our usual mutton and fowl. A curious lad waited on us—he was very open-eyed and solemn, his dignity was not to be disturbed by any amount of chaff. We called him Johnny, and spoke to him in any language that came handy, "Asht hazer bouka, donno me hongr?" (Is the food ready? we want to eat) was a sentence—half of which, by the way, is Sclav and half Albanian—which was frequently inflicted on him. "Yest, yest, hazer" (Yes, yes, it is ready) was the welcome answer he vouchsafed to us on our entry this evening. *Yest*, which literally signifies "It is," is the affirmative in this language, and at first surprises an Englishman by its resemblance to his native " yes."

CHAPTER XIII.

War preparations—Our camp visitors—An impromptu ball—
English Consul fashion—Robbers—Ruins of Douka—A
dangerous bath—Bastinado—Karatag yok mir.

THE following day we took a walk in the country, with our friend the armourer. The sheltered hollows literally swarmed with tortoises; one could count as many as sixty within the space of a few yards. A gap was pointed out in the distant hills behind the town, where was fought one of the most sanguinary battles of the last war—the battle of Medun—in which Prince Nikita gained a signal victory.

Our friend told us some wonderful story about a rich Turk who inhabited the present ministry of war some four years ago, before the war broke out. He was tyrant of Podgoritza, and forbade any one to bear arms in the town. This restriction seems to have excited the wrath of the Montenegrins, who were wont to come down to the Albanian city on market-day. Two of these daring highlanders came into the town one morning, concealing pistols on their persons. They met the aforesaid rich Turk in the bazaar, called him a dog and a thief, and thereupon blew his brains out.

The Mohammeddans then rose, and put every Montenegrin in the town to death—some twenty or thirty.

This, he said, was one of the causes which led to Prince Nikita's taking part in the Russo-Turkish war.

We had invited our new friend to sup with us. He seemed to appreciate fowl and mutton very well.

He gave us much interesting information as to the prospects of war and other matters. He said that artillery was already posted on the heights above Gussinje, and that the prince's troops would not be long in driving out the enemy. He told us he was not allowed to fight himself, his services as armourer being so exceedingly important. This was a source of great grief to him. In the last war he ran away from his work and joined the troops. The prince caught and rebuked him, sent him back to his forge, and told him to consider himself as a prisoner there. He once more sneaked down to the front during a great battle, his warlike ardour being too much for him. This time again the prince found him out, but could not refrain from laughing, and was obliged to pardon him.

The next day Robinson rode in with both horses. He had made rather a muddle of his errand, for having come down from Cettinje as far as Rieka, he then left Marco, to bring the tent and baggage on by londra to a place called Jabiak. It ultimately turned out that Jabiak was just as far from here as Rieka was. Brown rode off with a guide to this place, and then found the unhappy Marco sitting alone, disconsolate, tobaccoless, on the white elephant, mid the sedges by the shores of the lake, waiting till he should be called for. Brown described him as being an indescribably piteous object, as he meditated alone in that dismal swamp.

When, on the following day, Brown, Marco, the white elephant, and the two horses returned, we held a council; and though all unanimous in desiring to leave Podgoritza as soon as possible, could not decide as to whither we had best go until this dilatory war, which had been promised us by Robinson and Jones as an inducement to postpone our Albanian travels, should commence. As we discussed warmly the armourer came in, and said, "The minister of war wishes to see you as soon as you can give him an hour." "We can come now," we replied. So he ushered us into the reception-room of the war ministry, where sat the courteous and handsome old veteran, looking fully twenty years younger than he is. We sat on a divan, and were presented with coffee and cigarettes in the Turkish style. The armourer acted as interpreter, translating the general's words into German, which language both Jones and Robinson understood well. He said "he was exceedingly glad to see English travelling in his wild native country, and trusted we liked the people. Go all over it," he added; "you will be safe. Pilfering and highway robbery are quite unknown among us." On being questioned as to the preparations for war, he said, "It was to tell you about this I desired to see you. You wish to see the campaign: you shall do so. You shall come with me as my guests. My servants shall be yours. On no account leave the country just yet. What will be done will be worth your seeing." On being told that we were rather pressed for time, he went on to say, "Negotiations are pending at Constantinople. In four days we shall know all. Come to me then, and 1 can tell the very hour we march. That war will be, I am certain. The Albanians are sure to resist. Prince Nikita too has sworn to take Gussinje. It is his by treaty. We will take it, and no quarter will we give the dogs. Why should we? They are rebels. Turkey says she has given up the place to us, and that it is not her fault if the inhabitants resist. We will not spare one of them. If you wish to see something of the country before you see me again, go to Douka, where the great ruins are—they are worth visiting—then you can return here."

This proposal pleased us, so the commissariat was sent out to procure a large quantity of raki, mutton, flour, and other necessaries. Robinson was anxious to try the white elephant as soon as possible, so it was determined to take one of our horses to bear our impedimenta, and march out to as near Douka as we could manage this afternoon, and then camp for the night.

Douka is situated on the right bank of the river Moracha, some miles above Podgoritza.

Our landlord came with us, for as the sun was setting we did not expect to march for more than an hour, and he wished to see us comfortably settled for the night. Marco we left behind.

We marched on the left bank of the Moracha, thus cutting off a long loop which the stream formed here, and by sunset had arrived at a spot just opposite to the ruins of Douka, the broad and foaming river dividing us from it.

We pitched our tent in the plain not far from the precipitous edge of the river. The white elephant certainly looked very imposing, and was very comfortable. We unpacked the horse, and arranged all our property in an orderly manner in our new home. Then our landlord rode back to Podgoritza. The sun was now setting over the western hills, so we lost no time in cutting down some of the brushwood, and making a large fire some ten yards from the entrance of the tent; the pot was then put on, and a tasty stew prepared of mutton, grease-meal, onions, pepper, and salt.

I do not know whether, in Montenegro, to pitch a tent and light a fire signifies a general invitation to the country-side to come and make merry and carouse, but that was the result on this occasion. As night set in, first one and then another armed highlander would drop in, walk into our tent in the calmest manner, quite *sans gêne*, shake us by the hand, with a " *Dobro Eutro Gospodina*," then sit down, roll himself a cigarette, and commence smoking. At first we thought these people rather cool, but they were so polite that it was evident they did not imagine their conduct to be in any way extraordinary.

At last a large crowd had assembled round our tent—a very curious people. Where they came from we could not imagine. Houses there were none in sight. They seemed to have no homes, no occupation. It was a matter of utter indifference to them where they were at any time, or where they slept. We were at this encampment for two days: all the time they remained outside the tent in a most contented matter. They were just as well there as anywhere else. After dinner we provided coffee and raki for our visitors.

Then an impromptu entertainment followed. Robinson and myself gave a conjuring entertainment for the amusement of the wild people. We sat at the remote end of the tent. About seventeen of the audience sat inside in a double row : these were the swells in the stalls. The gods outside filled up the open door and looked over each other's shoulders, in a compact and surging mass. The conjuring was much appreciated by our audience.

When we had exhausted our repertoire of tricks, all cleared out of the tent, which had become very stuffy. It was a magnificent night. The moon was rising over the distant mountains, and there was not a breath of air to stir the rising smoke. We piled up the fire and made up a glorious blaze, which threw a bright light on our fantastic visitors. They were all now very merry and boisterous. They wrestled, sang, and ran, like a lot of children. Why not get up a ball? proposed some one. It was a happy idea; every one fell into it with delight. With loud shouts and wild gestures they whirled round the fire hand-in-hand, treading energetically, almost fiercely, a measure of their own. There were two charming young ladies in the crowd, who were the decided belles of the ball—Neda and Zekitza. Zekitza made a great impression on Robinson's sensitive heart. She was a powerful young lady, for once she disagreed with one of her partners about something, and caught him a resounding slap, which felled him to the ground. She also wrestled with another youth, and easily laid him low. It was a curious scene; not the least curious object was the gallant Jones handing round refreshments—raw raki in a saucepan, which girls and all partook of freely.

"Verily," the Montenegrins must have thought, "these are consuls Inglesi, and they do things in right good English consul fashion."

It was rather difficult to get rid of our guests when we wished to turn in for the night. That any one should like privacy at times is incomprehensible to Montenegrin or Albanian highlanders. They walk into each other's huts, uninvited, at every hour of the night, to chat and drink coffee. They seem to need a very small amount of sleep. I found, in the cabins and khans we visited, it was the rule to turn in about twelve and be up again at two, jabbering and coffee drinking; for it is not that they have any work to do that these people are so early in rising. After all, when you have no dressing or washing to get through, getting up early becomes easier than when the complicated toilets and tubbings of the Anglo-Saxon are before you.

When we arose the next morning the cook was horrified to find that a saddle-bag, containing our mutton and tobacco, had disappeared in the night. A burglarious entrance must have been made into our tent while we slept. We remembered having seem two suspicious-looking young fellows prowling about the camp during the ball, who were evidently strangers to the rest of the Montenegrins present, and who seemed to be shunned by them as disreputable vagabonds. These doubtlessly were the thieves.

One of our visitors, seeing us searching for something, understood the state of affairs, and told us by signs he would soon recover our property. This we thought rather improbable; but he knew what he was promising, as events showed.

The peasantry kindly brought some provisions to our camp this morning. Tubs of veronica, a sort of sour milk, goat's-milk cheeses, and wheaten cakes.

As our tobacco had all been stolen, I mounted Rosso and galloped into Podgoritza, to procure some more. On my return to the camp we started for the ruins of Douka, all our new friends following us. Further up the stream an ancient man had a boat, in which he ferried us over, three or four at a time. The boat was very rickety, and overgrown with moss; the boatman of great age, ragged, and of exceeding ugliness. He and his craft irresistibly called up Charon and his Stygian ferry to our minds.

Douka was evidently a Roman city. The peasantry gave us several coins they had found among the ruins; these were of the time of Diocletian, and bore his effigy. There was not much to see—a few ruined walls, and some slabs bearing illegible inscriptions, were all we could find. The ruins were thickly overgrown with brushwood. However, I should say this place would repay the labours of an excavator, for it must have been a place of considerable importance once. We amused ourselves with some rifle practice, and then returned to camp.

This evening Brown did a very imprudent thing—he washed himself. He went down to the river, stripped, and jumped into a deep pool. We warned him, told him he might be misunderstood by the people; but he was obdurate.

Some Montenegrins on the other bank saw him. "What is it?" they said, for at first they could not believe it was a man. Who ever saw a man with his clothes off—in water, too?

They were about to fire at the mysterious object, when somehow they recognized it as a human being. They were evidently much puzzled to know what on earth he could be doing there. Was this a curious religious rite of the Inglezi church? Was it a mystic ceremony connected with witchcraft?

We were bound to make some explanation for

Brown, for we found the people fought very shy of him when he came out of the bath, and looked upon him with evident suspicion and dislike, so we put our fingers to our foreheads, shook our heads sadly, and intimated to them that our poor friend was not quite right in his mind.

The next morning we were awoke early by the sound of voices outside our tent. On looking out we found an officer of some rank, and several armed men, bringing two prisoners to us. These were the very two men we had suspected of stealing our mutton. Our saddle-bag and its contents were restored to us by the captors. They had tracked the fellows up into the mountains during the night, with the assistance of a bloodhound. The officer stayed to converse with us awhile in very limited Italian.

As for the prisoners, he merely turned to them, pointed towards Podgoritza, and said "Go." They obediently skulked off in the given direction, and awaited him in the bazaar.

We found afterwards that the poor fellows were sentenced to be bastinadoed, thirty cuts on the sole of the foot each, and were then imprisoned for some days in a sort of open prison or cage.

We had exhausted the charms of Douka, so packed our baggage, and marched back to Podgoritza. Robinson superintended the lowering of the tent. This was the sole occasion during the whole tour on which the white elephant was brought into use. It was afterwards mildly suggested to its inventor that it might be a question whether all the tribulation and expense attending its carriage was made up for by these two nights' encampment on the plains of the Moracha. He was silent on the subject.

On arriving at Podgoritza we at once called on the minister of war, to learn the latest news of the war. He had heard of our little adventure with the mutton pilferers.

He was much amused at our account of it. "Ah!" he said, "and I had only just told you that robbers were unknown in Montenegro." As to the war, he had no news to tell us. Orders to advance might come to-day, might not come for a month. He knew no more than we did.

We left him, and retired to our chamber at the khan. After dinner we were smoking silently and sulkily, when Brown, addressing Jones and Robinson, sternly said, "This war of yours is a fraud, you have brought us out here under false pretences." I joined in to assist my ally, and laid stress on the delights of Brown's and my own projected march to Janina, which we had put off to hunt this phantom war all over this uninteresting country.

After a warm discussion it was decided to

march back to Scutari on the morrow. I communicated our design to Marco. The worthy fellow's face broke into broad smiles, as he whispered hoarsely, " Good, monsor, good; *Karatag yok mir.* Montenegro no bonne, no bonne." He evidently did not feel comfortable among his hereditary enemies.

CHAPTER XIV.

An escort—A Turkish dinner-party—Brigands—Our sportsman —A chief of the League—Objects of the rebels—Achmet Agha—A meeting of the League—The Boulem-Bashi of Klementi—An Arnaut chieftain.

THE next day (Saturday, November 1st), after our black coffee, and the usual bustle attending the packing of our animals, we shouldered our rifles, and made a start. Our landlord insisted on our pouring down numerous glasses of raki in his house, and, according to the general custom over here, accompanied us to about half a mile or more from the town, when a halt was called. Then he produced a glass, and a large bottle of mastic, which had to be finished by us ere bidding a final adieu. We all highly approved of this good old custom.

It began to rain soon after we commenced our march, and the plain assumed very quickly that lake-like appearance which we had observed the last time we crossed it.

On arriving at the khan where we had slept

on our march to Podgoritza, we found in front of it a large encampment of Turkish soldiers. We entered the house to get some coffee, and were then pounced upon by some of the officers, who wished to see our passports, and learn who we were, and whither we were bound. They insisted on sending an escort of four men with us as far as Helm, for, as they told us, we were breaking through all the regulations laid down by the government for the security of travellers in journeying thus without zaptiehs. That travellers should be thus escorted we knew to be the rule throughout Turkey, but we evaded it whenever we could. In Albania such an escort is worse than useless. In the first place, the zaptiehs will not venture to go with you into the mountains, where the Arnauts would probably attack them for the sake of their arms; and on the other hand, their company is sure to make you very unpopular in every village you go through, for these defenders of the peace consider they have a legal right to requisition provisions, and all they want, without paying for them.

On reaching Helm we found that the provision boat had left, thus we were obliged to pass the night here. Robinson proposed that we should pitch our tent. While we were discussing the point a Turkish officer came up, and spoke to us in French. He pointed out a dismal stone house by the lake side, and told us that the commandant of the troops stationed here resided in it, and would be very glad if we would accept his hospitality for the night. We were all delighted, with the exception of Robinson, who sighed deeply—his beloved tent was not to be pitched after all.

We were shown into a rough, unfurnished room, and dinner was soon announced. We dined with the commandant and the French-speaking officer, Marco and a negro soldier waiting on us. It was a regular Turkish dinner—no chairs, no knives and forks. We had to squat down in Eastern fashion, and eat the savoury pilaf with our fingers. After dinner we entered into a lengthy conversation with the commandant, the other officer acting as interpreter. He hated Albania, and the Albanians. "Why," he said, "these dogs of Arnauts should be smoked out of their fastnesses. My soldiers dare not leave the camp; if a few of them stray a mile or two away, 'ping, ping,' a dozen bullets hiss about their ears. The beasts murder them for their rifles. We might as well be in an enemy's country at once. I advise you to be cautious in travelling among these mountains. It is really very unsafe."

The conversation turned on politics. The old soldier seemed very excited. "Ay!" he said, "all our friends have forsaken us; you English even are no longer allies of the Turk. And this being so, why should we do anything for you? why assist you? why listen any more to your counsels? I will tell you, by Allah! there is but one stick left that Turkey may lean on. Her only hope is in an alliance with the strong, with Russia; that is what it will come to, you will see."

"I am afraid you will find that Russia devours her allies."

The commandant laughed. "There is something in that," he said. "The truth is, that poor Turkey has no friends, and no hope. We shall have to leave your Europe, I fear; but I do not think you will find that Turkey, overrun by Sclavs, will be so much better than it is now."

The next morning our host ordered a special londra for us, and ordered his men to row us down to a point on the lake, whence we could march to Scutari before nightfall. Our crew of ragged soldiers, grim, half-starved, some of negro, some of Arab blood, brought us, in about two hours, to a sheltered little bay on the east shore of the lake. Our course had lain across a regular forest of half-submerged trees, which grew in fantastic shapes, and whose lower ends were thickly surrounded with sedge and water-plants. The effect was curious, not unlike those tropical swamps where vegetable life is so profuse and varied.

On landing we repacked Rosso and Effendi, and were just on the point of bidding adieu to our crew, and commencing our march, when an incident worthy of mention occurred.

With the exception of snipe, and such like small deer, we had come across little game in Albania. The *feræ naturæ* have little chance in this barren country, where war is frequent, peopled as it is too by men who never leave their thresholds without carrying their loaded guns with them. But now, however, the keen eye of Jones suddenly lighted upon a large and unknown bird, perched on a stump not fifteen yards from the shore. It was a curious and melancholy-looking creature, something like a mangy pelican with a moulting tail.

Now Jones, my readers will remember, had purchased an Arnaut gun at Scutari, an orthodox flint-locked *pushka*, with barrel as long as himself. This weapon had been strongly recommended by the vendor for sporting purposes. On inspecting it, Jones noticed the barrel was most decidedly bent. He pointed this out to the merchant. "Bent! Ah, that is nothing," said he; "easily remedied." So saying he inserted the barrel between two of the beams of his roof, bent it straight, squinted down it, and handed it back. "There you are! Excellent pushka!"

With this weapon Jones proceeded to slay the

mysterious bird on the stump. Marco and the soldiers, on observing his intentions, became very alarmed. "Do not shoot here," said our follower. "The noise will bring down the Arnauts upon us; they will kill us."

But the sporting instinct of the Englishman was up. Slowly and warily, with the lengthy pushka held out at full-cock, with finger on the trigger, Jones crept nearer and nearer to the lake's edge. His reputation as a mighty Nimrod in the stubble of his native land was at stake. All our reputations were at stake as Inglesi, and therefore of a race of sportsmen.

Silently, yet excitedly, the soldiers watched. The eyes of Marco gleamed as he looked round. He was proud of us. "Now, you look out; you watch," he whispered to the men. He nodded his head with a knowing nod, that unmistakably said, "You will see." And "I told you so!" was ready to jump from his lips as soon as the report of the gun awoke the echoes of the wilderness. Our Nimrod crouched down; there was a pause; a great suspense. Then his finger pulled the trigger; the lock snapped! There was a fizzing sound, as of those "devils" the schoolboy makes of damp powder. With the fizzing there rose a pale blue smoke from the pan. The bird heard the sound, looked round at the stranger and his fizzing instrument curiously for a time, then, having satisfied his curiosity, he deliberately shook himself, spread his rickety wings, and flew slowly and majestically over the lake. It was nearly out of sight when there was a report. The pushka went off with an imposing bang that awoke the echoes of the mountains. A roar of Homeric laughter burst from the assembly.

In the rainy season of Albania it becomes very difficult to preserve the powder in the pan of one's gun in a properly dry condition. After a few days it becomes a slow fuse. But Jones soon mastered the ways of his mighty pushka, and was fairly successful in his future sporting expeditions; for having carefully timed the fuse, his method was to take aim and fire at least ten minutes ere the game was even in sight.

It was pitch dark when we reached Scutari, and walked through the abominably roughly-paved streets to the Hotel Toshli, where the brothers received us with open arms.

The next morning we held a council, to decide whither we should wander next. We came to no immediate conclusion, as there was great diversity of opinion. As Robinson was expecting a remittance from London, we should most probably have to remain a few days at Scutari. Having nothing better to do, we persuaded our friend the gendarme to introduce us to a chief of the Albanian League, who was a friend of his.

The interview had to be arranged with caution, for, as our friend said, "They know here you have been to Montenegro, and may suspect your motives in wishing to question a member of the League."

It was settled that we should go to the gendarme's house in the afternoon; there the chief in question would meet us.

In the afternoon Jones and myself were shown by the gendarme's Miridite servant into a room, where, squatting on mats, coffee-drinking, were our friend and a shrewd-looking old Albanian Mussulman, with deeply-lined face, and anxious and restless eye. After the customary salutations I entered into conversation with him, the gendarme, as usual, acting as interpreter.

I told him the English wished to know what were the objects of the League.

"Our object," he said, "is to defend our countries against the enemies that surround us. The dogs of Montenegrin, the Servian and Greek swine, all wish to steal a portion of Albania; but, praise be to Allah, we are strong. The Albanians are brave; and guns and ammunition are not wanting."

He tried to sound me as to the views of England, for he thought this frontier dispute was absorbing all the attention of our countrymen. He said, "England is our friend. They all say here she has supplied the League with weapons and money."

That some power—most probably Turkey—has assisted the League in this way, is certain. But it is curious that all the Albanians I met were positive as to England being the friend in question.

The Government of Turkey does not find favour in the eyes of the Albanians. "The Turks!" cried out the chief, angrily, "what do they do for us? Tax us, rob us—that is all. These effeminate pashas, these farmers of customs, do nothing for us in return for what they steal. Can they defend us? protect us? No! They have sold us to the cursed giaours of the Karatag. I tell you we will have the Turk no more. The chiefs of the League have sworn it. Independence has been given to Montenegro—to Bulgaria. Albania shall have her independence, and the great powers shall recognize us. If not, we care not. Leave us alone; that is enough for us."

He had now worked himself up into a furious rage, and was almost choking with it; so he stopped, drank some sherbet, then turning suddenly to me, said, "What do you English think of Midhat Pasha?"

"He is much liked by us," I replied. "He is looked upon as one of the few honest and worthy Turkish officials."

He seemed very pleased at hearing this, and said, "What we wish is to create an independent Albanian principality, with this Midhat Pasha as our Prince—a principality under the protectorate of England. You will see we shall have it."

I asked him whether this League was a purely patriotic movement, or whether it was a religious one, confined to Mohammedans only.

"We are fighting for our independence," he replied. "There are as many Christians in the League as Mussulmen. You know the Christians here are of the Latin Church, and hate the Greek Christians as much as we Mohammedans do."

He told me that one party of the League were not averse to the occupation of Albania by some big power; not Russia, he said, nor Italy, nor Austria; but England or France. For his part he did not wish this.

With regard to the defence of Gussinje, he said, "We have 35,000 men there, who will fight to the death. The Montenegrins cannot take Gussinje. Why, they never yet have fought us in the plain. The beasts can fight well enough behind their own rocks, but they are cowards to attack. When the Skipitars raise their shout, and charge with the yataghan, the Karatags tremble; they turn, they fly. Then we pursue them, seize them by their long hair, and with a sweep of our blades cut off the beasts' heads. Ah! it is sweet to see." And turning sharply to me, "Why do not you go to Gussinje and see the fighting? Parties leave Scodra every night for the front. I will give you a letter to Ali Bey. He will welcome you as a brother."

The proposal was pleasing; Jones and myself at once agreed to accompany the next party to Gussinje. We knew that the expedition was rather a risky one. The garrison of Gussinje had been worked up to a high pitch of fanatical madness, and might treat us with little ceremony did they hear of our journey into the enemy's country. Under these circumstances we thought it better that two of our party alone should go to Gussinje, while the other two could make a sporting expedition into the mountains beyond the plains of Scutari.

The next morning accordingly, Brown and Robinson, taking Marco with them, shouldered their rifles, strapped their blankets on their shoulders, and marched off towards the Miridite mountains—a lofty and wild range, inhabited by the tribe of the same name, the most savage and desperate of all the Christian highland class, a race that has waged a perpetual war with the

Turk for centuries. The Miridites are exceedingly poor, in a condition of half starvation, for bodies of Turkish troops ever and anon make incursions into the debouchures of their valleys, driving off their flocks, burning their villages, and compelling them to fly for safety into the cold and utterly barren highlands.

The gendarme brought to our room at Toshli's, the morning of our friends' departure, another member of the League, a chief of influence. He slipped off his shoes at our door, and shuffled in, a short-legged, stout, dropsical old fellow, with not over-clean festinelle, and a four days' beard: he had the fierce eye which is the characteristic of the Northern Albanians. The shaven head too of the Mussulman lent a peculiar ferocity to his expression. I never cast eyes upon a more blood-thirsty-looking old scoundrel. "Will your friend take some coffee or sherbet?" I asked the gendarme. "He likes raki best," was the reply, "when no one is looking on. He is not a very strict Mohammedan in this respect." I found few Albanians indeed had very delicate consciences when raki was in question.

This gentleman, who was introduced to us as Achmet Agha Kouchi, kept a coffee-house in the Mohammedan quarter of the town. He purposed going to Gussinje in a few days, and would be pleased if we would accompany him.

We were to visit him at his café in the afternoon, to arrange matters.

After lunch we traversed the dismal streets of the Turkish quarter till we, reached the little café of our new friend. It was full of Leaguesmen, who had evidently come to inspect us. I wish I had taken a sketch of that interior. No slum of an Eastern city could show a group of more cutthroat-looking, fierce ruffians than those Scutarine conspirators.

They did not rise when we entered, but stared at us with savage, lowering looks, that betokened suspicion and hatred of the giaour.

Achmet Agha told us that a party would start the night after next for Gussinje; and that to-night there would be a meeting of the Scutarine Leaguesmen, in the mosque near the river, to decide whether we should be permitted to visit the besieged town.

In the morning he would let us know what had been decided.

In Toshli's this evening, I read an account in a Trieste paper of a battle which had been fought near Gussinje, in which the Albanians had been victorious. Rumours of all kinds had for days been flying about the bazaar; but though Gussinje is but a three days' march from here, nothing certain was known. Indeed the Scutarines were entirely without information on the progress of matters.

Some excitement was caused by the departure of Mr. Green to-day for Cettinje. He had of course gone thither to take a part in the negotiations now pending, the Turks having sent a representative to the Montenegrin capital, to try his utmost to arrive at an amicable solution of the difficulty. The Scutarines, however, were quite certain that Signor Green had gone off to threaten Prince Nikita with an immediate declaration of war on the part of England, did he not without delay withdraw his troops from the frontier.

The League met as usual at midnight, in the mosque, and till daybreak discussed Jones and myself. The meeting was described to us. Said some: "Let them not go; who knows that some of the men of Gussinje will not murder them as giaours? Then what difficulty we shall be in. We will have to avenge them, for they are our guests; there will be strife between the defenders of our country, and the dogs of Karatag will rejoice. Again, their blood will be upon our heads. Zutni Green will be wrath. The English will be our friends no longer."

However, the dissentients were in the minority. The League of Scutari gave its permission to our departure.

We were advised to wear the fez instead of our English hats, as this would reduce the risk of our irritating the intensely excited habitants of Gussinje: accordingly we purchased two of the orthodox head-coverings.

Achmet Agha again called on us; he seemed rather uncomfortable. We could see he had heard something about us, and did not like to carry out his promise. Said he: "Who are you? Why do you wish to go to Gussinje?" We replied: "In England we will write a book. The English wish to know what the Albanian League means, whether it is good. It is for that we wish to go to Gussinje, that we may see, and be able to tell our countrymen the truth." "Ah," he said, "so your 'krail,' your chiefs, have sent you for this. *Mir, mir*—it is good."

Then he paused, and said abruptly, "We shall not go to-morrow."

"Why not?"

"Because we know not how the other Leaguesmen will receive you. We must first send to inquire of our general, Ali Bey, if he will have you."

This did not sound very pleasant to us. Ultimately he agreed to take us on the morrow to a hut two hours distant from Gussinje; there he would leave us while he rode into the town, to acquaint the chieftains with our wishes, and obtain permission for us to visit Ali Bey.

The next morning we rose at daybreak, and found a strong "bora" was blowing, and the snow lay thick on the distant mountains.

We prepared for the start.

Luggage we took none, except one blanket; but as it promised to be exceedingly cold in the mountains, we each put on two flannel shirts and two pairs of socks.

Achmet Agha called two hours after his time; he seemed confused and troubled. Our host, Toshli, came forward as interpreter, for I managed to make out a good deal he said. With him I conversed in a strange mixture of Italian and Greek, one of the *six* compound tongues I had to invent in Albania in order to get on with the different people I met.

Said Achmet Agha, "I cannot go with you. I have been told by the authorities that if anything happens to you I shall be held responsible; my house and property will all be confiscated. Besides, I have to tell you that you are forbidden on any account to go to Gussinje; the pasha will not have it." This all seemed very strange. That the Turkish pasha and police authorities should have acted thus seemed improbable. We afterwards found they did not even know anything about our intended journey.

We did, however, hear something later on, which led us to very strongly suspect that the attempt to stop us originated in a certain foreign consulate at Scutari.

Naturally suspicious and jealous of English

influence in Turkey, the representatives of this power concluded that our government had sent us here on some secret errand; and so, not being able to discover the object of our mission, attempted to frustrate it altogether in an underhand manner.

Jones and myself had now thoroughly made up our minds that we would go to Gussinje, in spite of an over-officious consul, so we proceeded to hunt about Scutari for a guide and dragoman.

No one could we find. Those we spoke to smiled grimly, drew their hands significantly across their throats, and emphatically objected to go anywhere near the hot little town.

One person, however, did volunteer to accompany us. This was the English Consul's cook. He was a plucky little Albanian, very vivacious and clever. He spoke two words of nearly every language in Europe, and in default of better, would make a very fair dragoman for us. He had adopted European costume, and wore jauntily on his head an English army forage cap, the gift of the British sergeant who accompanied the frontier commissioners last May. This cook was a man of some rank. In Albania, a calling such as was his is not derogatory to a gentleman. We had made his acquaintance at Toshli's, where he was famed for his skill as a billiard-player. He went to Mrs. Green, told her of our intended journey, and implored her to give him leave of absence, in order that he might guide and protect the Inglezi travellers. Alas! It could not be; his presence was indispensable in the consulate kitchen. Cooks are not to be picked up every day in Scutari, at any rate such cooks as this, for we had several opportunities of perceiving how skilled he was in his profession, under Mr. Green's hospitable roof.

No one to be found to come with us! This looked bad; we almost despaired of effecting our purpose, for to find our way alone across the roadless mountains would have been impossible. To have travelled among the savage Arnauts, without knowing ten words of their language—madness.

As we discontentedly discussed the question in our bedroom, the head cavasse of the English Consulate was announced. He brought with him a tall, handsome, and very pleasant-looking Albanian Mussulman, evidently a man of high rank, superbly dressed and armed. "This," said the cavasse, "is the Boulim-Bashi of Klementi. He will accompany you to Klementi, which is a day's march from Gussinje. There he will hand you over to the chieftain of the Klementi, Nik Leka, who is a friend of Signor Green. He will say to Nik Leka, these are friends of Signor Green; treat them as his brothers, and if the danger be not too great take them to Ali Bey."

My readers can imagine our delight. We could not travel under better auspices. The condition of a boulim-bashi is curious. The Turks, as I have before said, have never really conquered or assimilated Albania; the Christian highlanders are allowed considerable independence. Now, each Arnaut tribe is obliged to elect from the Mussulmen of Scutari a representative, a sort of consul, who mediates between it and the Turkish Government, who acts as their advocate in case of any dispute. As he is chosen by the tribe from among the townsmen of rank, and as he can be dismissed any day if the highlanders in any way object to him, the boulim-bashi is always a popular man, liked by the tribe he represents, and a very safe person in whose company to travel among the highlands, for he is sure to be known to, and treated as a friend, by every man met on the way. It was a great honour to be thus escorted, and we afterwards discovered, the cause that led to the kind proposal. The men of Klementi are deeply indebted to our consul, who took their part in a certain quarrel between them and the Turkish Government, in which justice was entirely on their side. Grateful for this, the Klementis are ever glad to do any service for Zutni Green. Thus it was that we as friends of the consul received this invitation. The Klementi is the most powerful tribe of this district. There are

6000 fighting men, all armed with Martini-Henry rifles, stolen from the Turks. Their chieftain, Nik Leka, to whom the boulim-bashi was to escort us, is the hero of the Scutarine Christians. The timid townspeople of the Latin faith, unarmed as they are by law, live in fear of the Mohammedan population, who have more than once fallen on and massacred them. It is to the armed Arnauts of the hills, their fellow-Christians, that they look for protection, for these are better warriors than the Mussulmen themselves, never have been a subject race, but stalk, bristling with arms, through the bazaars of the cities on market-days, as erect and haughty as the most blue-blooded young Mohammedan emir of them all.

This Nik Leka had a little adventure recently in the bazaar of Scutari. He was discussing some matter with a young Mussulman of rank, who had three retainers with him. A quarrel ensued. The other called the Arnaut chief a dog of a Christian. Nik Leka is a man of few words. He whipped out his yataghan with his right hand, seized his enemy by the little tail of hair which the faithful leave on their closely-shaven heads to give Mahomet something to lay hold on when he pulls them into Paradise, and the next moment there was a flash of bright steel, and the Arnaut held up a bleeding head, while the body fell into the foul gutter below. The man's retainers fell upon Nik Leka, but the wiry highlander was too much for the effeminate townsmen. He slew two of them, the third escaped; then he picked up the three heads with a grim smile, tucked them under his arms, and marched off to his mountains, where he exhibited the ghastly trophies to the tribesmen.

CHAPTER XV.

To Gussinje—The valley of the Drin—A rough road—In the mountains—Hospitality—A pretty woman—A scientific frontier—Franciscans—Dog Latin—Marco Milano.

IT was settled that we should start early on the following morning. Then the boulim-bashi bowed low, shook hands, and left us. We had learnt something of the nature of the place we were about to visit from Mr. Green and others. About three days' march from Scutari, across the great Klementi mountains, there is a long and beautiful valley, which penetrates deeply into the central range of the Mount Scardus. Down this valley flows the White Drin, a stream of considerable importance, that flows into the Adriatic, near Alessio. In this valley are Ipek, Jakova, and Priserin, three of the most interesting cities of Albania, inhabited by a population very skilled in the working of metals. The most beautiful saddlery, filigree work, gold-hilted and jewelled yataghans and pistols, are here worked by an industrious people.

But the population of these towns is ferociously fanatical. Surrounded as they are by Christians, knowing that the day is not far off when the rising ambitions and energies of the oppressed race will drive them from their homes eastwards and southwards, the Mohammedans here hate the Christians with a hatred more intense than even the followers of this fanatical creed entertain in other parts. At the very head of this valley of the Drin, where the river springs out from the grey rock, is a ridge of forest-clad mountain, the ancient Pindus, which forms the watershed of the tributaries of the westward-flowing Drin, and Bojana, and the Lim, a river that flows northwards, joining the Drina and the Save, across Bosnia and Servia, till it ultimately pours its waters into the mighty Danube at Belgrade. At the head of the valley of the Lim, situated in the centre of a green and fertile *cirque*, surrounded by stupendous mountains, is the little town or village of Gussinje, a congregation of sordid wooden huts. It is a place of great strategic importance, for just behind it, on the ridge of the forest-clad mountains, Montenegro, Bosnia, and Albania join.

By the provisions of the treaty of Berlin, Gussinje and its neighbourhood was handed over to the Black Mountaineers—wherefore it is difficult to see.

As conquerors in the war, it seems just enough

that the Montenegrins should have acquired
Antivari by that treaty, a place of no strategic
importance, yet which gave them what they so
long and eagerly thirsted for, a seaport. But it
was decidedly a mistake to extend Prince Nikita's
territory beyond the mountain ridge, a natural
frontier, down into the valley of the Lim, giving
a command of it—a standing menace to Turkey
and Bosnia, a bone of many future conten-
tions. It must be remembered, too, that the
inhabitants of the district to be given up are not
Sclav in race or language—not of the Greek church
—but Mussulmen or Roman Catholics. The Montenegrins have been made too much of lately.
They now imagine that they are a great people,
and have a holy mission of aggrandisement at the
expense of Turkey.

Gussinje is a curious sort of a place, and has
never enjoyed a very sweet reputation. As in all
parts of Northern Albania, the people do pretty
much what they like, and do not feel the Turkish
yoke very heavily. Situated as it is on the frontier, it has become a city of refuge. Montenegrin
renegades whose country has become too hot for
them, Bosnian Mohammedan refugees, and vagabonds of all sorts, have flocked hither. It is in
this town of Gussinje that the chiefs of the Albanian League have concentrated their forces,
determined to fight to the bitter end, in spite of

the Austrian troops in Bosnia to the north of them, Turkish troops in their rear, Montenegrins before their walls, and the doubtful neutrality of the Christian Arnauts, who are all round them in the mountains, lying in wait to murder and strip small parties of either side—for this is the idea of neutrality among these people, an armed neutrality with a vengeance. Thirty-five thousand Albanians, we were told, occupy Gussinje, at the head of whom is Ali Bey.

Ali Pasha, as he has styled himself, is a Gussinian of rank, owner of lands and houses in the town and neighbourhood, a man of great intelligence, and a devout Mussulman.

He was one of the principal people implicated in the assassination of Mehemet Ali at Jakova.

This general, as my readers will remember, was sent by the Porte on the dangerous mission of negotiating the transfer of Turkish territory to her enemies. He was strongly advised not to venture into that hotbed of fanaticism and fierce patriotism, Jakova. The League held possession of the town; the population was worked up to the highest pitch of excitement; every one knew the history of the envoy. As a foreigner, a Pasha's favourite boy, a renegade, he was certain to be disliked and suspected by rigid Mussulmen, and was the very last man that should have been sent on so delicate an errand. It is rumoured that the jealousy of his enemies at Constantinople sent him on this surely fatal journey.

His death was decided on by the League. The projected murder was talked about freely in the bazaars of Albania fully two weeks before it was perpetrated. Contrary to advice, he entered Jakova. He had not long been there before the house in which he and his companions were shut up, was besieged by a furious mob. One man, a Franciscan father, whom I met at Scutari, was with him, and managed to escape, disguised as an Arnaut.

Mehemet, seeing that resistance was hopeless, died like a brave man. He opened a door, rushed out, unarmed, with hands stretched out, into the thick of his enemies, crying, "Kill me, but spare the others." He was beheaded, and his head was stuck on a pole, and held up to the jeerings and desecrations of the populace.

We were up at daybreak the next day. It was a sunny, exhilarating morning, that seemed to send fresh blood coursing through our veins as we mounted Rosso and Effendi, and rode through the Mohammedan quarter to the house of the boulim-bashi. Our luggage was simple enough. I had one blanket and my waterproof, strapped behind me on Effendi's saddle; while Jones carried, in the same way, a saddle-bag of provisions and his waterproof. The house of the boulim-bashi was enclosed within lofty walls, as are all the residences of the Mussulmen. We were ushered into a large room, where the brother of the boulim-bashi received us smiling, and motioned to us to be seated on the luxurious cushions which were strewed on the thickly-carpeted floor. He was a tall and very handsome man, like most of his countrymen, possessing small, delicately cut features, and tiny hands and feet. He looked like an aristocrat, and his costume was exceedingly rich.

The boulim-bashi came in with coffee and sherbets. He had thrown off the dress of the town, with its ample festinelle and rich linen, and had donned the simpler dress of the Arnaut chieftain, which showed off his fine person to great advantage. His cartridge-boxes betokened the man of rank, being of gold, beautifully worked, as were the handles of the pistols in his variegated silken sash. The coffee was prepared over a silver brazier on the floor, and the cups were handed to us on trays, covered with napkins cleverly embroidered in coloured silk and golden thread. We found that we were expected to take these napkins away with us. We did not know the custom, but our host soon set us right.

There is something particularly pleasing and refined in the manners of the high-caste Albanians. Their politeness is charming; they anticipate your every want; and their movements have a cat-like softness, noiselessness, and suppleness about them, which is very striking.

The boulim-bashi seized his Martini-Henry, leapt on his horse, an active-looking little grey, with undocked mane and tail.

We were soon out of the town, and then broke into a canter, which we kept up across the plain of Scutari till we reached our old friend the khan, at Koplik.

We felt very jolly this morning. We had made a start. There was a spice of adventure and risk in this expedition, that lent it zest, and excited us. How we were to get on at Gussinje we did not know: our guide spoke no language but his own. It was improbable that we should find any one in the mountains who could understand us. And again, how would Ali Bey and his men treat us. We had no valid excuse for visiting him. Would they know that we had interviewed the prince and war minister of Montenegro? If so, our reception might prove almost too warm. We trusted to luck, and determined to see all we could.

At Koplik we left the track by the lake, and turned to the right, towards the desolate and lofty mountain range.

These were the very mountains that the Turks at Helm seemed so afraid of, as being inhabited by the fiercest and bravest of the Arnaut tribes, addicted to plundering Turk and Montenegrin indiscriminately. With our friend, the representative of the tribe, we were, however, quite safe, certain of being received with every hospitality; and as friends of Zutni Green, every man of the tribe would be friendly to us. For the Arnaut is very grateful, is never treacherous—and once a friend is always a friend, and an excellent friend too.

We gradually reached the foot of the mountains, and then our route lay through the heart of them, for to reach Klementi we had to cross this stupendous chain. For seven hours we were nearly constantly ascending. There was no pretence at a road. We had often to dismount to haul our horses up a higher block of rock than usual, and had to use the greatest care, as we rode along some track not two feet wide with a wall of rock on one side and a precipice a thousand feet in depth on the other.

The shades of night were falling—it would be impossible to travel after dark on such a route. But the boulim-bashi had timed himself well. It was just dusk when we heard that welcome sound to the traveller—the baying of dogs. Our guide signed to us to dismount. We led our horses down an incline, when suddenly a door opened, and a blaze of light fell on us and dazzled our eyes. A gigantic Arnaut, gun in hand, came out suspiciously. He at once recognized our companion, and kissed him affectionately.

On hearing that we were English, friends of Zutni Green, he shook us kindly by the hand, and bid us enter.

"Bramiamir. Mir s'erd" (A good night to you. Be welcome) were the salutations we exchanged on entering the house. Then, according to Albanian custom, we unstrapped our arms, and handed them to our host (a sign of confidence in a friend), who proceeded to suspend them with his own on the wall.

We were seated on mats by the blazing fire, and the women pulled off our boots. It was a curious scene, highly interesting, and taking one very far indeed from Europe and civilization. A large room, the walls of rough stone, admitting the wind freely; the roof of huge, rough-hewn rafters of larch—wall and roof blackened with smoke; the floor of clay; in the centre a fire of great logs, the smoke allowed to find an exit as it could, the result being very unpleasant to unaccustomed eyes; no lamps or rushlights, but a pale and flickering light given out from a sort of iron cup, supported on a rod, into which little chips of resinous wood are occasionally thrown; the walls decorated with arms, the only ornaments in the place. A few cups, a bowl, an iron pan, and one or two other utensils, complete the *ménage*. This is the house of a great man, a chieftain; and we were told the name of the place is Castrati. A large family occupied the hut, for it was no more. There were several women and young men.

By the fireside there sat a very old crone, who paid no attention to what was going on, but rocked her palsied body too and fro, and mumbled constantly to herself. A little child— maybe a great-great-grandchild—whose sturdy limbs were a strong contrast to the withered legs and arms of the old woman, sat by her side. The grandame attempted now and then to stroke the little thing's head, the only sign she showed of being conscious of the world around her. All the occupants of the hut were remarkably handsome. Leslie, who so well delineates pretty childhood, should visit Albania. I verily believe no children in the world are so beautiful as these little Arnauts. Their costume is not graceful. A woollen sack is thrown over them, and their arms and legs are thickly swathed with the same material.

They are quaint little things, and the smallest has the proud, fearless, free carriage of his fine race. There was one little fellow who stood in front of us here, erect, with head well up, and hands behind his back. He stared at us for a long time with big, wondering eyes, and a wonderful smile at the corners of the mouth, and then came boldly up to investigate the material of our clothing, which was evidently new to the little mountaineer.

Dinner was soon prepared. The boulim-bashi had brought some sweet cakes with him, and some mutton, which he cut into small lumps, and stuck on a skewer. They looked for all the world like catsmeat; but, when peppered, salted, and grilled in the glowing fire, they turned out those sweet and succulent morsels so appreciated by every old campaigner, known under the name of "kybobs." According to Eastern custom the wife of the master of the house poured water over our hands from an iron jar, and then we commenced to devour our dinner with our fingers, washing it down with excellent raki.

This lady of the house, by-the-bye, created a great impression on both our hearts. She was indeed exceedingly comely. Her figure had not been spoiled by labour, as are those of most of the countrywomen, nor by the want of exercise and cramped sitting position in which the legs soon lose their shape, as is the case with most of the townswomen. Her legs were bare, not swathed in the ugly manner in usage when out of doors, and very shapely legs and ankles she possessed. Her face was oval, of a rich carnation in tint. Her mouth small, and very beautiful; but her eyes were her chief feature—long, almond-shaped, and with a voluptuous dreaminess in them. Their length owed nothing to the artificial blackening of their corners with henna. She saw we admired her, and was evidently pleased. She laughed, and made eyes at us throughout the evening; and at night, when all the inmates of the room rolled themselves up in their blankets, and stretched themselves round the fire in a circle, feet to the blaze, she brought us some mats for pillows, and tucked us in very nicely with her delicate fingers.

"Bothmir, mik" (Good health, friends), was the frequent challenge of our jovial host. He insisted on our drinking a fair amount of raki. He was not backward himself; I am sorry to say even an Arnaut will get drunk upon occasion. After dinner a happy thought struck me. I rose, and plunging my hand into our saddle-bag, produced a bottle of brandy we had brought with us from Scutari. This was a great and unaccustomed luxury to the Arnauts. I do not think they had ever tasted it before. They smacked their lips over it, and repeatedly said, " Raki Inglesi mir, mir " (The English raki is good).

At last to bed. Comfortably rolled up in blankets, in spite of insects—we did not mind anything in that line now—we slept till daybreak.

The boulim-bashi then awoke us. The fire was raked up, coffee was made, our horses were saddled, the stirrup-cup was drunk over our good-byes to our friends, and we were off.

The Arnauts are very proud. It would be a grievous insult to offer a man money in return for his hospitality. The proper thing to do is to distribute what you intend to give among the children. When you are gone, the mother goes round and collects it from her offspring; it is then put away, to be expended in sugar, salt, and other necessaries, on the next market-day at Scutari.

At this great elevation the morning was bitterly cold. The aspect was very desolate—a wilderness of rock and stone, with scanty vegetation. Far away, thousands of feet beneath us, stretched the white sheet of the Lake of Scutari, looking cold in the early morning, with the bleak grey Montenegrin mountains in the background.

From sunrise to sunset we rode over the trackless and almost inaccessible mountains. We met several men during the day, fine and fierce-looking members of the Klementi tribe. Every one had a Martini-Henry rifle and a belt of cartridges. The stories we had heard of these people from the Turks at Helm were evidently true; these weapons had never been bought. Indeed their owners had little idea of their value. One mountaineer we met pointed to his rifle, and said,

"Inghilterra, sa paré?" signifying that he wished to know what was its value in England. On hearing the amount he seemed much astonished, smiled grimly, stroked the weapon, and said, "Ah! the Skipitar get them for less than that."

Such an abundance of cartridges have these highlanders managed to steal that it is a common sight to see a shepherd firing his rifle in the air, at frequent intervals, to drive his sheep. The people we passed all stopped, and questioned the boulim-bashi as to who we were, and whither we were bound. On hearing that Gussinje was our destination they looked surprised, and made that clicking noise with the tongue and teeth which with us signifies pity or annoyance—in Albania, mere wonder or admiration. The sign language of this people is so utterly different from ours that it is impossible to get on with them at first. For instance, they do not shake the head when they wish to refuse anything, but bow and wave the hand, in a manner which would lead any one to imagine they meant to accept.

It was evident they all looked on us as doomed if we entered Gussinje. So far I could not make out whether they sympathized with the rebels or not.

Towards midday we reached the summit of the range, and on turning a bluff of rock there lay beneath us one of the most magnificent gorges I had ever seen, even in the Alps. The great mountain was rent into a profound ravine, whose sides were nearly perpendicular. There were places where the precipice ran down sheer, for 4000 feet at least. Where there was any footing, grand larches and beeches, tinted with the golden shades of autumn, covered the slopes. Far below one heard the roar of the great torrent, but a purple haze lay at the bottom of the gorge, and concealed the foaming waters. This ravine forms the frontier of Montenegro and Albania. As Jones suggested, a very scientific-looking frontier too.

Our destination, the village of Klementi, was situated on the edge of the torrent, some miles higher up the valley. We now had to descend ⁀n the mountain to the bottom of the ravine. ⁀ous descent it was. The path, a mere zigzagged down the precipice. It ⁀ary to dismount, and watch the horses ⁀. They stumbled every moment, and ⁀ther than walked. In places the path ⁀d give a sharp turn, and here the boulim- ⁀shi would hold on to each animal's tail as he passed the awkward corner, to prevent him going right over the edge. There were some very nasty bits, and even these mountain horses trembled with nervousness at times.

We passed a house on the bank of the torrent

in the afternoon. The whole family came out to see the travellers. These people were friends of our companion. The men came out, shook hands with us, and then entered into an animated conversation with the boulim-bashi on the subject of the war. While we sat on our saddles outside the house the women brought to us refreshments, apples, cakes, and raki, first taking our hands and kissing them respectfully.

This was a very long day's journey. Now riding, and now walking, we ascended the ravine, fording the torrent several times, whenever one or the other side of it afforded the better path.

The scenery was grand, but desolate; in the higher portion of the valley the forests that clothed the lower end were wanting. Great walls of rock fell sheer into the turbulent stream; and in places great fan-shaped slopes of débris—masses of mountain broken up by hurricanes—jutted out across the gorge, damming up the waters into profound pools. These gigantic wastes of black stone, streaked as they were by patches of snow in strong contrast with their whiteness, gave an impressive weirdness and desolation to the scenery.

About an hour after dark we halted before a large two-storied hut. "*Scpiia Nik Leka,*" said the boulim-bashi—the house of Nik Leka. Here, then, we were at last in the stronghold of the notorious Arnaut chieftain. We entered the large lower room, which in every respect was similar to that in which we passed the previous night at Castrati. There were at least fifteen people squatting round the fire—men, women, and children. A tall, splendidly-built, and very handsome man came up and greeted us. He was about fifty years of age, very dark, with a much-lined, sad-looking face. He had fine black eyes, deeply sunk, and surmounted by bushy black eyebrows. There was something exceedingly frank and noble in his look—a man one could trust.

This turned out to be the brother of Nik Leka, and, as we afterwards found, much resembled that chieftain. We sat down by the fire, and all were busy in attending to our comforts, when a door opened, and, to our astonishment, there bustled in a jolly-looking little fat Franciscan monk, a very Friar Tuck. He wore the brown frock and girdle of his order; but, like all the Franciscan missionaries in Turkey, his head was covered with a fez. He was followed by a quaint, lean, smiling old Arnaut with a lamp, a simple, goodnatured-looking being—the faithful old servant of the mission; he had been for forty years in the service of the Franciscans.

The friar came up to us and shook us by the hands in a most cordial manner. "Come up to the mission," he said; "come up to the mission, and stay with us. Ah! what joy to see Europeans up in our wilderness! Come along!" and he fairly dragged us off.

Not thirty yards distant was the mission-house, a very comfortable establishment for this country —a low building, with a small church adjoining it. At the door we were met by the three other brothers, as cordial and jolly as the first.

Never did traveller fall into better hands. They all bustled about, jabbering and laughing incessantly, doing all they could for our comfort. Maccaroni and mutton kybobs were soon prepared; and they stood round, pressing us to eat, and helping us to abundant portions as we sat at the table.

I have seldom heard men laugh so heartily and boisterously as did our jolly hosts. The feeblest joke set them off in a roar. "This," said the fat little Father Luigi, pointing to the smiling servant, "this is our Lord Mayor; he looks after our corporation—ha! ha! ha!"

The dinner over, we sat down over pipes and coffee, and talked for half the night. They were really glad to see us; never were strangers so quickly made at home as we were. Of course the conversation soon turned on the object of our journey.

"Go to Gussinje!" said Father John; "impossible! You cannot go. Why they will at once cut your throat. These Turchi at Gussinje are animals—beasts—swine. O, my dear brother Edouardo, you must not go. Why, even we dare not go there; the Arnauts dare not go. Nik Leka went there three days ago, to see Ali Bey; for that beast desires an alliance with the Klementi. Nik Leka has not returned; we fear they have killed him. If so, God help this country; for the Klementis will take their guns and yataghans, and march on Gussinje to avenge their chief."

This did not sound very encouraging to us; but we had come so far that we did not relish the idea of abandoning our project now. We knew the timid monks would most probably, with very good intentions, exaggerate the dangers. As they were the only people we could converse with, we saw it would be necessary to impress them with the absolute necessity of our progressing, else they would lend us no assistance in what they considered to be a fatal journey.

Our four hosts were Italians; Luigi came from Turin, John from Naples, and the two others from Modena. I am not a proficient at Italian, so we conversed in dog Latin, putting in an Italian word now and then, when we could not call up the Latin equivalent. It was a curious mixture, but we got on fairly well with it. I had a little conversation with Jones; he was as determined as myself to visit Gussinje if at all feasible; so we decided to dissimulate a little, in order to obtain the very necessary assistance of our friends.

I said, " I know to go to Gussinje is dangerous— very dangerous possibly; but we have been sent to see Ali Bey at all hazards, and must not go back without doing so. We have friends at Gussinje, and I do not think we run so much risk as you imagine."

The worthy monks now, of course, concluded that we were political envoys; that our mission was secret, and not to be divulged to them; but that its object was to settle the Gussinje difficulty and hinder bloodshed.

They then saw that we were right in insisting in running the risk, for it was our duty to do so. They would do likewise in our place. They looked very sad, shook their heads, and said, "Ah, my brothers, but you go to a certain death. However, as you must go, we will help you; we will write a letter in Arnaut to Ali Bey, asking whether he will see you, and send men to escort you to the town. The brother of Nik Leka will take the letter. To-morrow you can ride to the hut of Gropa, in the mountain; it is but two hours from Gussinje. There you can await the reply."

The letter was written. I did not quite like

the idea of playing the amateur diplomatist in this way; but we had gone too far to go back now, and without doing this there was no chance of our seeing Gussinje.

The missionaries evidently looked upon and admired us as noble martyrs, sacrificing our lives to duty. They insisted on our drinking an abundance of wine. I suppose they thought this was our last chance of so doing. We found from them (and what they said was confirmed by others) that we had been greatly misinformed by the leaguesmen of Scutari as to the strength and nature of the organization. There were not 35,000 men at Gussinje, but between 6000 and 7000. These were all Mussulmen—Albanians and Bosnian refugees, and deserters from the Turkish army—a frightful rabble, the scum of this part of Europe. Artillery they had none.

They told us that an army of 10,000 Montenegrins, with some field artillery, was encamped in a strong position, not two hours' march from Gussinje.

The general of the Black Mountaineers was Marco Milano, a man who has already made himself a name in former wars. Of him, most probably, the world will hear more some day. From all accounts he is a man of uncommon ability, one of those strong characters that inspire confidence in all whom they come across. He is an Albanian by birth, from the neighbourhood of Gussinje. Irritated by some injustice he had received at the hands of the Turks, he fled from his native land, and took refuge in the Black Mountain, where his talents soon brought him to the front. As a renegade always is, he is the bitterest foe to his race, and his voice is ever for a policy of war and aggression. This, at any rate, is his reputation in Albania.

As for the Catholic Arnauts, who the Scutarines told us were fighting for the league, not one of these people sympathized with the insurgents in the slightest degree. They knew too well that if these Mussulmen succeeded in their projects it would go hard with the Christians. At this time the mollahs in Gussinje had taken up arms, and were exciting the population to religious frenzy, preaching the death of all infidels. Ali Bey, a wise man, was indeed working hard to gain as allies the powerful Arnaut tribes. He had invited Nik Leka, the most influential chieftain of the north, to Gussinje for this object. "Nik Leka," said Padre Luigi, " will talk to him—talk as much as Ali likes—he is a regular diplomat; but fight for the beasts of Turchi—not he. He may promise to allow bands of men to go unmolested through these mountains on their way to Gussinje, but he will want an equivalent for that. The Arnauts hate the Montenegrins and Turchi alike;

most probably they will shoot and plunder detached parties of both sides."

The missionaries spoke very highly of the Christian highlanders.

"Ah! they have many virtues," they said. "Good friends, good fathers, good husbands; kind to each other, truthful, hospitable, never treacherous; they are a noble people. But," continued Luigi with a sigh, "they are such savages, so utterly indifferent to human life. They have but one absorbing vice, and that is their love of murder."

This cruel vendetta of theirs, which decimates the population, is horrible. There are no really old men. Every man is murdered sooner or later. It is thus they wish to die. To die in bed is a disgrace. In battle they behead their own wounded friends; this is looked on as a favour; for to survive, maimed and unfit for war, would bring lasting reproach on a warrior and his family.

Nik Leka's brother walked off with the letter for Ali Bey at midnight. He carefully loaded his pistols and rifle before starting.

CHAPTER XVI.

The mission-house — Gropa — The mandolin — A letter from Ali Bey — A trap — Our throats in danger — Retreat — Nik Leka — Proverbs — A pleasant evening.

THE next morning we were up early. The good priests would not hear of our leaving them till after the midday meal. "Gropa is but three hours or so from here," they said; " you have lots of time to stay and look over our church."

The little mission-house of Selz, as this the chief hamlet of the Klementi is called, is built on a terrace in the hill side, which commands a grand view of the ravine; gigantic bare cliffs of dark stone shut it in on every side. A small graveyard, where are buried all the monks that have died since the institution of the mission, lies to the front of the residence.

We went inside the little chapel. Very primitive and rough paintings of Biblical incidents ornamented the walls, the productions of the monks. Most of these were some 200 years old at least. The Franciscans have undoubtedly done much good in Albania. They have been here from a very remote time. They have suffered persecutions, have died the death of martyrs, but have succeeded in completely winning the affections of the wild Arnauts. As Luigi said to me, "Why, should one of us be ill-used by the Turks, the whole of the mountains would rise in our defence. We need fear nothing here now." The headquarters of the order in Albania is at Scutari, where there is a large convent. I was much struck by the evidently sincere respect and love all the mountaineers entertained for their spiritual fathers. One could see that these men must be doing good here.

Before we started for Gropa, the snow began to fall heavily. We bid adieu to our good hosts. They kissed us and wept over us, for they feared we should never return, and insisted on filling our saddle-bag with wine, maize, bread, and mutton. Gropa, which signifies in the Albanian tongue the hollow, is not a village, but a miserable one-roomed hut, situated at the extreme end of the ravine, by the source of the torrent.

The path was coated with ice, and very perilous for the horses. Our guide, a savage-looking Klementi, walked bare-footed over the sharp stones and frozen snow with utter indifference.

The hut was nearly snowed up when we reached it. It was a desolate spot. A black pine-wood rose behind it on the hill-side. An hour's walk through this would have brought us to the summit of the ridge which overlooks Gussinje. The hut was inhabited by a man, his wife, and one child. A blazing fire was made up; then converting our mutton into kybobs, we made a capital dinner. They gave us coffee, but sugar they had none. Our guide, who had lately walked bare-footed over the ice quite at his ease all the time, now placed his feet in the ashes of the fire with a like indifference. Extremities of heat and cold affected the hardy highlander very little.

Our host was a musician in his way. He took down his mandolin, and with it accompanied one of the monotonous songs of his country. The Albanian mandolin is like a small banjo with three strings, and is played not with the fingers, but a chip of hard wood or bone.

These Albanian songs are not unpleasing, barbarous as is their music. The first line of each verse is the same as the last line of the preceding verse. There is a peculiar sadness and subdued fierceness in the way they sing which is really very affecting. The song is always of war, of victories over the Karatag, feuds with the Turk, or the doings of the heroic Scanderbeg. The mandolin is peculiar to Albania. The guzla of Montenegro has but one string, and is played with a bow like a violin.

At midnight we were awakened by the entry of two men. One was the brother of Nik Leka; the other a Bosnian Mussulman, by his dress. The Arnaut clapped me on the back. "Mir, Mir," he said, "Gussinje." Then he pointed to a letter. I understood what he meant. Ali Bey had given his permission, had written a letter to the fathers to that effect, and had sent this Bosnian soldier with it to Seltz. The soldier returned to Gussinje at once, while Nik Leka's brother also left us, to carry the epistle to the Franciscan mission. All seemed now to be going well, and very delighted we were. We should see Gussinje after all.

It was early the next morning, when Father John suddenly made his appearance at the hut. He looked alarmed and anxious, and talked rapidly to our host. Something unpleasant had evidently occurred. We waited patiently till he vouchsafed to explain matters.

"I have heard from Ali Bey," he said. "Here is his letter. I will translate it to you. He writes thus:—

"'To Father John, greeting.

"'We have read—we have understood. The chiefs have assembled. If these people will be hostages, will guarantee that Marco Milano withdraw the Karatags within three days, let them

come to Gussinje; if not, they had better not come.
"' From ALI PASHA.' "

This was hardly what could be called a hearty welcome. Said John, "You understand what that means. If you can guarantee that the Montenegrins withdraw their troops—"

" We cannot do that."

" Of course not. Well, if you go they will wait three days, then cut off your heads. Now Nik Leka's brother has also brought this news from Gussinje. When they heard of your arrival, some of the men said, ' We have heard of these people. They have been to Podgoritza; they are friends of the Montenegrin chiefs. They must be spies. One is a red-bearded Russian (this was Jones). They are accursed giaour traitors.' Then thirty men decided to leave Gussinje last night, and surprise and murder you here in this hut. Ali Bey heard of it, and stopped them. But Nik Leka's brother says that you had better not stay here. The Gussinians are violently excited about you; they thirst for your blood. Come back to Seltz."

We were sitting down to breakfast when we heard all this cheering and appetizing information. My back was to the door, as was Jones's, when I heard a noise outside, and the next moment I saw the Franciscan drop the meat he was holding, turn very pale, and stare in a frightened way in that direction. I turned; the doorway was blocked up by two men, evidently two of the defenders of Gussinje—one in Bosnian dress, one in Albanian festinelle. Both were armed to the teeth. Their faces were not prepossessing. There was a fierce, stern look in their eyes, which wandered anxiously and fiercely round the hut, and a determined expression in their tightly compressed lips, which meant mischief. Whether more were behind, we could not yet see.

Jones and myself were unarmed. According to the custom of the country, we had delivered our revolvers over to our host. He too, and also the priest, were without weapons. The two parties looked at each other without speaking for a moment or two. Our host's wife took her child by the hand, and looked steadily on with compressed lips, to see what would happen next. An Arnaut woman is familiar with bloodshed. However, bloodshed was not intended, it seemed. "We are envoys from Ali Pasha," said the Albanian. "Come in, then," said our host, suspiciously.

They entered, but seemed ill at ease, and suspicious of foul play. However, we made no advance towards our arms, and keeping a sharp eye on the men, continued to eat our kybobs. They sat by us.

The Albanian went on, the Franciscan translating,—" Ali Bey will see these Englishmen, but he does not wish them to enter the town; he cannot rely on his men. Ali Bey is but one man; he cannot protect them, if some wish evil to these men. Ali Bey and the chiefs will therefore meet them outside the town. Let them come with us."

It seemed improbable that Ali should have sent these men with another message, so soon after the first. The Albanian is deliberate in counsel, and does not alter his mind in this way as a rule.

" Do not go," whispered the Franciscan. " Do not believe them; there is some treachery." After what we had heard, we thought our friend might be right, therefore we refused to avail ourselves of their escort. Their faces fell. They talked long and eagerly to the priest and our host.

The priest said to me, "Listen to what I say, but show no surprise or alarm. Let them not think I am telling you this. They are talking to our host about you. They say you are spies, and they are endeavouring to raise his suspicions of you; they mean you evil. O amici," he said in his dog Latin, " multum est periculum per vos."

I now entered into an explanation of our journey. I showed that it was the most natural thing in the world that we had visited Montenegro; and soon disarmed any suspicion our host entertained; but the two Gussinians stuck to the point. The Bosnian turned fiercely to the Arnaut. "By Allah," he said, "they are spies. We have twenty friends in the hills behind here; since they will not come with us, we will kill them here; now is the time." I remember the very words in which Father John, with pale face, translated this to us: "Ille homo," he said, "dixit ad alium, Nunc est tempus intercidere illos homines." The Arnaut spoke. He stood up in his hut with quiet dignity, and without showing the least excitement said, "These are my guests. You think that I will assist you to kill them. They are my friends; I will defend them. Now you are armed; we are not. Possibly you may kill us; but remember, it is nearly three hours to Gussinje. Men of our tribe have seen you approach; rest assured there are many rifles of the Klementi among the rocks. If you wish to go to Ali Bey, and not rot on the Klementi hill-sides, you had better go in peace." The men looked at each other in silence; they knew the words of the Arnaut were true, and not being yet weary of existence, swallowed their coffee and sulkily left the hut. We took our revolvers and went outside, to see if any others were in sight. There were none; but on a rock that commanded an extensive view, we saw the erect form of a white-clad Arnaut, rifle in hand, scanning the ridge of the hill. The Klementis had evidently kept their eyes open. The probability is that these men had left Gussinje without the permission or cognizance of Ali Bey, and hoped with a fabricated message from the chieftain to tempt us to follow them to some spot, away from our friends the Klementis, where an ambush lay in wait for us. In their annoyance at our refusal to accompany them, they had betrayed their object.

No sooner was this adventure concluded than the occupants of the hut sat down and continued their coffee-drinking and smoking, as if nothing had happened.

Little events of this kind are every day occurrences in this wild country, and are thought nothing of.

The woman put her hand to her throat and drew it backwards and forwards, then laughed merrily, evidently chaffing us about the two separate risks we had so recently run of losing our heads.

As it was now evident that the people of Gussinje were not very anxious to entertain us, we saw there was nothing left but to return to Scutari. We were very disappointed; but what could we do?

We rode back with Father John to Seltz. The missionaries and the Lord Mayor rushed out. They were delighted to see us return in safety. "Ah! Frater Edouardo, Frater Athol, come in.

My poor friends, come in and sit down. How alarmed you must have been. Fear not; here you are safe."

During dinner our story was repeated over and over again by the gesticulative little Father John, and great was the commiseration expressed for us by the kind-hearted fellows. The Lord Mayor became very warlike. "Had they hurt you, I would have taken a gun, gone to Gussinje, and shot Ali Bey—that devil!—myself," he shouted.

While we sat round the fire after our meal, the door opened. "Nik Leka!" joyfully cried out our hosts, "Nik Leka safe! Praise be to the Lord."

The celebrated Arnaut chieftain stalked in smiling, kissed each father on the cheek, shook us warmly by the hand, and sat down by the fire. He was very like his brother, a splendid specimen of a barbarian warrior; very handsome, with an expression that curiously combined great good-nature with a certain amount of latent ferocity.

He corroborated all we had heard about the feelings entertained towards us at Gussinje, and said, "You would not live long were you in that *ferri*—that hell over the mountains." He himself had been obliged to escape, for his life was in danger among the fanatical inhabitants.

"They are like madmen," he said, "now—starving, desperate."

He expressed intense hatred of the *Turkis*, as

the Albanians call all Mohammedans. "Devils," he said, "robbers. '*Ku Turku vee kambet atu sdel baar*' (Where the Turk puts his foot, the grass grows not)."

Nik Leka has one vanity—he likes to be called a diplomatist. Talk to him on politics, the handsome warrior puts on a very knowing and wise expression.

Our conversation ran very much on politics to-night.

The fathers said, "These Arnauts have one wish. They know that an Albanian autonomy means Mussulman fanaticism, war, and Christians driven from the plain to starve in the mountains. What they wish is, that you English would take the country. All the mountaineers discuss this and desire it. So too do the Christian townsmen. Do you think England will occupy Albania?"

This was a poser. I did not like to say England would never dream of doing such a thing, and that Austria would have a word to say in the matter, so merely pleaded ignorance as to the counsels of my country. Nik Leka nodded his head when my response was translated to him, smiled and winked at me, as much as to say, "Ah, these priests don't understand politics. We diplomatists hold our tongues."

Nik Leka told us that our old friend the bullying Bekir Kyochi, for so is spelt a name pronounced as Bektsé Tchotché, was in Gussinje with the leaguesmen. "I should say the Scutarines will not weep much if the Montenegrins take his head," I said. "Ah," wisely replied the chieftain, "we say in Albania, '*Ana e kecie nuk schet*'" (The worthless pot does not break).

Nik Leka, I found, considered that the discourse of a great diplomatist should be liberally interspersed with pithy saws and proverbs. He rolled them out with unction, and repeated each two or three times till he arrived at what he considered to be a properly emphatic delivery.

He told us he would accompany us back to Scutari; we should start early on the morrow. We were in luck; we had travelled hither with the boulim-bashi of the tribe, we were to return with its head man. We conversed till a very late hour. "A veritable Tower of Babel," said Father John, with his stentorian roar. Latin, Albanian, Italian, Sclav, and English words were flying about the room, to the utter confusion of the Lord Mayor, who sat, looking very wise and sleepy, trying to make out what on earth it all meant.

I rose very high in the estimation of Nik Leka, when he heard that it was in Latin I conversed with the fathers. I was a greater diplomatist than ever in his eyes. He was a curious fellow. He would look at me thoughtfully, then suddenly jump up, shake me violently by the hand, and cry, "*Mik, Mik*" (You are my friend; you are my friend)—and then burst out laughing.

A very jovial evening we all spent over the log fire, drinking the fathers' wine and raki.

CHAPTER XVII.

Rosso and Effendi—A barbaric feast—Patoulis—Mead—The future of Albania—The Italia Irridenta—Sport in Meriditia—Dick Deadeye.

VERY warm and affectionate were our farewells on the morrow, when we left the good Franciscans. "Ah!" said Luigi, "it is a sad thing thus to make friends, and so soon part for ever. We may meet perhaps in some other remote land. For we Franciscans are ever changing the scene of our labour—now here, now there; in the deserts, in the teeming cities; but always *in regionibus infidelium.*"

We saddled and mounted our horses, and commenced our ride down the ravine. Nik Leka walked; he carried with him two long pistols and a Martini-Henry rifle, all, I observed, at full cock. This was all the luggage he took with him. Honour should be given where honour is due. Never did member of the equine race behave so well as did the fat little Effendi and the lean and haggard Rosso. For twelve hours out of the twenty-four from dark to dark, for six consecutive days, did these worthy animals carry us over this wilderness of rock and ice. Fodder was scarce. Rosso lived chiefly on the rare bits of timber he met on the way. He did not care much for live trees, but had a preference for the more tasty, decayed fallen wood. He was a *gourmand* in his way.

Effendi had a more delicate stomach; a diet of fresh fallen snow had greater charms for him than any other. We found they were of one mind, or rather stomach, in their intense relishing of maize bread.

Our return journey was rendered difficult and dangerous by the frozen snow which covered the mountains. However, just as the sun was setting we approached the hut of Castrati.

Half a mile from it we passed a woman. She stopped, and spoke to us. We at once recognized the pretty, smiling face. It was our old friend the wife of the owner of the house. She ran on before us to apprize her husband of our arrival. Nik Leka evidently saw that we admired the lady. He was much tickled, slapped me on the shoulder, and said, " Castrati mir " (Nice place, Castrati).

" Ah," I said, " Grue Castrati fort mir " (The women of Castrati very nice).

The chieftain roared with laughter. My remark

was repeated over and over again in the hut this evening, and much amused every one.

On entering the hospitable house, our host and all the other inhabitants of it came forward, and gave us a very cordial welcome. They were genuinely glad to see us back safe. Nik Leka told our story. They laughed, pointed to their throats, and shook us by the hands. Our pretty hostess, speaking broken Albanian, so that we might understand her, added, " Gussinje yok mir, Castrati mir."

A lot of neighbours came in. Every one was bustling about; preparations were being evidently made for a grand feast in our honour.

The old crone in the corner was just where we had left her; I don't suppose she had moved since. She was awakened from her lethargy by the unwonted hubbub, looked peevishly round now and then, and mumbled savagely.

I must describe this evening's feast in full, so characteristic was it. The fire, as I before said, was lit in the middle of the mud floor, the smoke escaping as it could. Huge logs—I ought rather to say trees—were now piled on. A tremendous blaze was made up.

When we entered, the fire was low, a loaf of maize cooking in the embers.

The method of making these loaves is simple. When the fire has burnt long, and the floor beneath is thoroughly hot, the ashes are scraped away in the centre, the loaf is placed on the bare mud, and an iron cover, which fits closely to it, placed above it. Then the hot ashes are once more raked back till they entirely bury the loaf and its cover; and the baking commences.

Our host went out and killed the fatted sheep, and proceeded to prepare it for roasting whole. A slit was made down the belly, the entrails were taken out, the feet were tucked into the slit, which was then carefully sewed up, and a wooden spit was run right through the carcase from head to tail.

It was brought in and placed over the fire. The spit worked on two rough logs, one of the women turning it with her hand.

We commenced our dinner by coffee drinking. There is certainly but one way of making coffee—that in vogue in these regions. Let my readers attend to this receipt, and try it.

On the fire is a pot of boiling water. A small saucepan, with a long handle, just big enough to hold a coffee cup of water is taken (N.B. a small Turkish coffee cup). Into it is thrown a teaspoonful of coffee, freshly ground and freshly roasted, also a lump of sugar.

Boiling water is poured on it till the saucepan is full. Then the saucepan is put on the fire. It boils over, is taken off for ten seconds. Three times this operation is repeated, then the thick fluid is poured into the cup; and delicious it will be found to be, if you once get over your prejudice against grounds. We and all the other men squatted on our rugs round the blazing fire and roasting sheep, and commenced our dinner, the women, according to Eastern fashion, standing or sitting in the corners of the room, watching us, and waiting till we had done, when they would come in for their share of the feast. The old crone was a favoured person; a bone was occasionally thrown to her by the host while we dined, which she seized in her skeleton hands, and sucked greedily with her toothless chaps.

There was a knowing old dog by her who knew, and took a mean advantage of, her blindness and weakness, for he managed occasionally to steal a succulent morsel out of her very hands.

While the sheep was roasting we were obliged to eat little delicacies, intended, I suppose, to tickle our appetites. Our host would take "patoulis" from the ashes of the fire (a sort of rancid, heavy dripping cake), smear them thickly with honey, then on the top of all scatter large lumps of goat's-milk cheese, and hand them to us in a pressing way that permitted no refusal.

We were forced to eat so many of these that the roasting sheep, of which we knew we would have to partake freely, turned before our eyes like a horrid nightmare. Meanwhile Nik Leka looked on benignantly as he put away the cakes in a way that surprised us.

We washed down all this with a very greasy sort of mead. Though of a fairly omnibibant nature, we could hardly stomach this. At last we came to the "*misch i pickun*," as the roasted sheep is called. Our host cut it up with his yataghan, then proceeded to tear the flesh with his fingers. We were well looked after, and treated as honoured guests. The Arnaut would pull off some rich lump of fat, enclosing a kidney, and hand it to one of us. The meat was really very good; all its richness is kept in by this way of cooking, but probably a delicate-stomached person might not relish the idea of devouring lumps of tepid mutton fat with his fingers, without bread or salt.

I think I did very creditably at this meal. I know Jones, who finally collapsed and could do no more, looked at me with amazement. Fat and lean and crackling followed each other. Our host and Nik Leka did not leave me alone for a moment. Now and then one of them would tear off a large shred of meat, and stuff it into our saddle-bag for the next day's provision.

At last we were as replete as Homer's heroes. Indeed the whole scene carried one back to those days. The besiegers of Troy lit the fire of logs, and roasted the beasts whole, and ate till they could not stand or talk, just as did these no less savage Arnauts. Just like these too, when the banquet was over, did they show their gratitude to their host, and appreciation of his hospitality, by frequent hiccups and belchings.

The women and dogs gobbled up the remains in their corner, as we smoked our cigarettes and toasted ourselves in old raki.

We were up before daylight the next morning. It had snowed heavily in the night, so our descent to the plain was slow, and not unattended with danger. Our good-byes at Castrati before starting were affectionate and protracted. "*Me teneson miku idaxtun!*" (Good-bye, dear friends), were the last words of our pretty hostess, as she waved her hand to her departing admirers.

At the khan of Koplik, where we were beginning to be well known (this was our fourth visit to it), we lunched off the fragments of the sheep which our host had thrown into our saddle-bags in the exuberance of his hospitality on the previous night. It was dark long before we entered the intricate lanes of the faubourg of Scutari. So here we were once again, having failed in our attempt to reach Gussinje. However, the expedition had not been altogether a vain one. We had seen a good deal of the manners and customs of the Arnaut; had journeyed away from the main roads into the heart of the great mountains, where,

I believe, none of our countrymen had ever ventured before; and again, we had learnt a good deal more of the real strength of the league than a month's inquiries at Scutari could have taught us. Not that I did not take the Franciscans' account with a few grains of salt. The fathers hated the Mussulmen, and were anxious to withdraw our sympathies from the defenders of Gussinje.

The world will hear a good deal of the doings of this Albanian League some day, so a few remarks on what, from my observations, I consider to be the real condition of affairs, will not, I think, be here out of place.

The chiefs of the association are, I believe, honest men, patriotic, and determined to carry out their programme to the death.

Ali Bey is spoken very highly of even by the Montenegrins, and if reports prove true, will show himself no indifferent general.

Nearly every Mussulman in Albania is a member of the league, and its forces are daily swollen by refugees from Bosnia and deserters from the Turkish army.

That Turkey at first secretly assisted and encouraged the movement, I think there can be no doubt. At any rate it is certain that the Porte's representatives, even her highest officers in this country, openly sympathized with it.

But the league has waxed too strong for the

government, who could not crush it now were it desirous of doing so. The leaguesmen, feeling their strength, have extended their programme. Defence of their native land against foreign invasion is now not their only cry, but Autonomy, and the shaking off of the Turkish yoke are boldly discussed in the bazaars of the garrison towns.

The Montenegrin difficulty may be settled; the principality may agree to take some lands near Antivari in lieu of the Gussinje and Plava district; but there are other and more serious complications behind.

To resist the advances of Austria on the north and Greece on the south are the avowed objects of the league. It is only too probable that the dual empire will be compelled to carry her arms into this province; for a lawless, fanatical, self-ruling Albania will be far too troublesome and dangerous a neighbour for her disaffected Bosnia. An occupation of Albania is confidently spoken of by all the Austrian officers I met in Dalmatia.

But an invasion of this country will be no mere military promenade. As mountainous, and as easy of defence as Montenegro—inhabited by at least as warlike a race, and better armed, Albania may prove as hard a nut to crack, as the Black Mountain has proved to Turkey, who for hundreds of years has in vain hurled army after army to perish on those grey rocks.

I think there can be little doubt, too, that the Christian Arnauts will join the league, in case of any invasion. They, too, love their independence—for independent they practically are, the Turkish yoke never having been felt in these wild hills.

Passionately fond of war, poor and starving, as the highlanders have been since the Turco-Russian war, the certainty of plunder, if nothing else, would compel them to join one side or the other, —and which that side would be it is not difficult to say. That the Turks can effectually interfere is quite impossible. Any one who knows how high-strung the Mussulman sentiment now is, how insubordinate the generally obedient ill-treated Turkish soldier has now become, can easily foresee what would be the natural result of a Turkish general leading his men to fight against their co-religionists, in order to force them to deliver their country to the giaour. They would mutiny, lay down their arms, fraternize with the men they had been incited to slay. It would be the tale of Mehemet Ali over again.

I see some wild story went the round of the European papers, to the effect that Muktar Pasha had led a force against Gussinje, and had been assassinated. As a matter of fact he was, to my knowledge, nowhere near Gussinje at the time. But such would be the fate of any commander who led Turkish troops on so unholy an errand.

The Montenegrins have openly declared that they will treat the soldiers of the league as rebels, giving no quarter. They are very sanguine; but in my opinion if the Black Mountaineers and the Albanians are allowed to settle their quarrel by themselves, no other power intervening, we may hear of Ali Bay at Cettinje, before we hear of Marco Milano at Gussinje.

How the Albanian difficulty will end it is difficult to see. That the troubles of this lawless province of Turkey may indirectly lead to serious complications is more than likely.

Beyond the Adriatic, too, lies another power, that is eagerly watching the progress of matters —Italy.

The Italia Irridenta party is very anxious that the government should lay a claim to Albania, when the day of Turkey's dismemberment comes.

All Italians consider that their country has been slighted and left in the cold in the recent adjustment of oriental affairs. The Austrians, without striking a blow, have acquired Bosnia and Herzegovina. England and France have assumed a sort of protectorate over Egypt, even Greece has gained territory.

That Italy is casting covetous eyes on Albania is certain; and equally certain is it, that she would be seriously annoyed if Austria should occupy the whole eastern Adriatic shore, from Trieste to the Ægean.

In Albania, one half of the inhabitants are Roman Catholics. The priests, who here have great influence, are all Italians by birth.

These are accused of intriguing in the interest of their government, of sowing seeds of rebellion among their flocks. On this point I am not capable of giving an opinion. The Franciscan missionaries I met seemed to be anything but friendly disposed towards the rulers of their native land.

That the Italians have carried on intrigues down the whole East Adriatic coast is certain. At the present moment the Albanian League are in doubt whether to offer the princedom of their country, when they have liberated it, to Ali Pasha, Midhat Pasha, or to a prince of the house of Savoy. Whatever may eventuate, there is one thing very certain; this is, that neither Mussulman nor Christian in Albania are likely ever again to take up arms in defence of the Turkish Government. They are sick of it.

The Mohammedans see that it is impotent to forward their interests in any way. The Arnauts, who fought well for Turkey in the last war, have been treated with great ingratitude ever since. They will only fight in the future in independent defence of their country against the foreigner.

If we are to believe the latest news from these regions; most of the Christian clans have at last decided to join the league. When I was in the country they were in a wavering and undecided state.

If this news be true, there is every prospect of a long-protracted and ferocious war, for the Albanians are a terrible foe, and not easily to be crushed when they once rise in earnest to defend their country, as history has more than once showed. With such a leader as Ali Pasha seems to be—of great ability, of intense zeal, ambitious to be a second Scanderbeg—the autonomy of Albania may not be far off, and probably may not be so very undesirable a thing.

For here we have a people in religion, sentiment, and race, utterly differing from those Greeks and Sclavs, to whose mercies Mr. Gladstone would like to see their native land delivered. They are a people quite apart from the other eastern Adriatic peoples—a noble race, that deserves its opportunity quite as much as do Montenegro and Bulgaria. This question is attracting little attention now, but I should not be surprised to find that before long this attempt of a brave people to acquire its independence will gain the sympathies of the English.

Ingratitude is not an Albanian vice. It might happen that an Albanian principality might prove, in some future time, an ally not to be despised.

I will conclude these remarks by once more repeating, that any one who travels in these countries with unbiassed mind must be of opinion that the Albanians are quite as likely—to say the least of it—to prove capable of self-government, as are any of the southern Sclav peoples, and that unless it be deemed best that Austria, or some other great power, occupy the country, it would be well that autonomy were granted to them, and exceedingly unwise to deliver them over to Greece and the neighbouring Slav states, who have quite enough to do in looking after their own affairs.

On arriving at Toshli's, Brown, Robinson, our landlords, and other friends, expressed their delight, and even astonishment, at seeing us once more with our heads securely planted on our shoulders.

We exchanged experiences with Brown and Robinson. They chaffed us a little on our failure in Gussinje; but we found that we could return the compliment. When they left us for the Miridite mountains they (Robinson especially) were exceedingly sanguine as to the success of their sporting expedition. They would return to

Scutari with a train of mules laden with the skins of the beasts they had slain. They were going to make such a bag as had never been heard of in Albania.

Now that they had returned they were remarkably reserved as to their doings in the mountains. They came back empty-handed—of course because they could not procure horses to carry the spoil.

At last—first from one, and then from the other—the true story leaked out. Their sport had been a dismal failure. They found that the highlands were, to say the least, chilly at this late season.

Marco struck, and would proceed no further into the snow-covered wilderness, for our Arnaut follower had a liking for warmth, and a not unnatural hatred and fear of the fierce brigands of the Meriditia, who are the terror of all the country in the vicinity of their mountain fastnesses.

Under these circumstances they returned to the lowlands, and visited the seaport of Alessio, and some other neighbouring towns. The chief events of their expedition were the great hospitality they received from a Roman Catholic bishop in one place, and from a self-elected pasha, an ex-brigand, in another.

Another follower had been added to our party during our absence. This was one of those

Bohemian dogs one occasionally comes across in cities. A disreputable improvident, albeit clever and good-natured animal. He had a profound contempt for orientals, and we were told invariably made the acquaintance of any Europeans who visited Scutari. He generally managed to pick up something at the consulates, but lived a very hand-to-mouth sort of life; he was liked as a jolly fellow by the decent dogs of Scutari. If any canine that ever prided himself on his respectability scorned to associate with him, he, at any rate, had cause to repent, if he audibly expressed his disgust in the vagabond's presence. When the frontier commission was in Albania, this dog attached himself to the English delegates, and was by them named "Dick Deadeye," from his striking personal resemblance to that discontented mariner on board H.M.S. "Pinafore." Dick Deadeye was out of town when we were last at Scutari; but as soon as he returned and heard that Englishmen were in the town, he hurried off to Toshli's, called on Robinson and Brown, and kindly offered to accompany us whithersoever we might wish to go.

A very affectionate old friend he turned out to be; very useful, too. When the savage Albanian dogs would rush out from some wayside farm-house to yelp at the strangers' heels, Dick Deadeye would soon settle them.

The season was now far advanced; snow fell nearly every other day; and it was evident that it would be difficult, and very unpleasant, to travel further in this roadless country this year. Some of our party, too, wished to be in London by Christmas. So, after holding a somewhat stormy counsel, we decided to leave Scutari in three days' time, and march to the port of Dulcigno, where we should just arrive in time to meet the coasting steamer from Corfu to Trieste.

CHAPTER XVIII.

The coffin—A pasha's death—Horse-dealing—The postman—Brigands—An hotel bill—Down the Bojana—Dulcigno—Pirates—Farewell.

WE spent these last three days in purchasing arms and other curiosities. Between us we collected a very arsenal of strange weapons of every kind. A carpenter at the bazaar constructed a box for us in which to pack them. This box was about six feet in length, and somewhat more than two feet in breadth. It looked uncommonly like a coffin. The ever-ingenious Robinson, when it arrived at Toshli's spent a whole evening in painting a ghastly-looking mummy on the cover, and other horrible ornaments on its sides. As may be imagined, it created some interest on our journey.

The day after our return to Scutari the pasha very suddenly died, whereupon the whole city rejoiced much and openly, and indulged in more raki than was good for it.

The doctors attributed his decease to apoplexy.

It seems he had drunk a cup of coffee, when suddenly he complained of intense pain, and vomited. In ten minutes he was no more. Turkish pashas are strangely subject to this curious and fatal illness, which, in nearly all cases, follows the drinking of a cup of coffee or sherbet.

Perhaps it is in consequence of the well-known antipathy between these beverages and the pashaic stomach that so many of these distinguished men have taken to Veuve Cliquot, notwithstanding the Koran's strict ordinance. No one in Scutari for a moment doubted that poison was the true cause of the mysterious complaint. Of course there was no post-mortem. The Mussulman has a superstitious objection to any mutilation of the human body, in life or death.

Our faithful companions, Rosso and Effendi, had next to be sold. We marched them up and down the bazaar day after day, Marco loudly dilating on their many virtues. No one seemed very anxious to purchase at our price. The dealer who had sold us Rosso offered us one-fifth of the sum we had paid for him originally. Yet we had decidedly improved the animal's condition.

At last we managed to sell Effendi to the Austrian consul. But Rosso hung on our hands to the very morning of our departure. No one would have him at any price, even his original owner retracted his offer. Should we be obliged to leave the poor animal a homeless vagabond, to wander about the streets of Scutari in search of a master, begging for crusts to keep life within those pathetic ribs? It seemed like it.

Brown, in despair, wandered through the alleys of the bazaar, eagerly informing the merchants that he had a red horse for sale.

"Rosso Vendetta," as he expressed it, which, if it means anything, means a sanguinary blood-feud. The quiet Christian merchants must have imagined that the Englishman was running amuck, and was about to slaughter them all.

At the last moment the khanji of the khan where Rosso was lodged and fed came to us, and offered us 200 piastres—about 30s.—for our noble steed. We had to accept it, for the animal was hardly worth taking to England with us.

It was a bright sunny morning when we bid a final adieu to our numerous friends at Scutari, and started for the coast. We had sent the coffin and our other baggage on in advance, on the backs of the mules of the British consulate postman. There is no post-office or postal service of any kind in North Albania, so letters are sent to the coast in this way, to be taken up by the passing steamers.

The office of letter-carrier is of some importance in this country, for it is in the gift of the government, the carriers having the monopoly of the transport of all goods from town to town. As there are no roads, and hence no carts in North Albania, everything has to be carried on the backs of horses or mules; this of course accounts for the very high prices of all imported goods.

Each carrier owns some twenty horses, and his calling would be an exceedingly lucrative one were it not for the heavy black-mail levied on him by the brigands.

The carrier to Dulcigno to whom we had entrusted our baggage, had, we were told, been stopped on his road three times within the last few months.

The whole business is managed very quietly. On some lonely portion of the way, a picturesque gentleman, armed to the teeth, suddenly appears, and in few words persuades the drivers to deliver up their charge. These in a philosophically resigned manner accept their ill-luck; discussion they know would be useless, as the muzzles of several long Albanian guns peep ominously from the rocks above.

We paid Toshli's bill, which was quite a curiosity in its way.

Our landlord had been to some conventual school in his youth, and had acquired the rudiments of the classic tongues. He now utilized his knowledge, by setting down the many items of his account in what he imagined was Latin.

Occasionally, where his memory of that language failed him, he would put down the name of some comestible in Greek.

He must have taken great trouble in the composition of this document; he came up with it smiling, evidently very proud of it, and remarked that as we did not understand Albanian, he had done his best to make it intelligible for us.

The total looked enormous, calculated as it was in piastres, more like a national debt than an hotel bill. We shuddered as we contemplated the four figures of the total. However, a little calculation showed us that we were not about to be burdened with an impossible debt, which might keep us here in pawn for the rest of our days.

The port of Dulcigno is situated half a day's march north of the mouth of the Bojana, the river that takes off the waters of the Lake of Scutari to the sea.

The pleasantest way of making the journey, we were told, was to descend the river by boat to a certain bend near the sea, and thence go on on foot.

We accordingly hired a londra which lay alongside the quay by the bazaar.

Our landlords, the Boulem-Bashi of Klementi, and some of our other friends, came to see us off. After a good deal of hand shaking the four Englishmen, Marco, Dick Deadeye, and two Albanian boatmen, embarked, and we were soon descending the river on the top of a strong current.

It would be a very good speculation to run a small steamer to Scutari.

The navigation of the Bojana is easy, and the imports into Scutari from abroad are considerable. But I suppose this would be an infringement of the monopoly granted to the carriers; and it will be long ere the authorities perceive the advantages of this mode of transport over the slow, expensive, and dangerous carriage on the backs of mules and horses, across a land unprovided with roads.

Dick Deadeye was in a very melancholy state of mind during this voyage. He lost his appetite, and grumbled to himself a good deal.

He had before this descended the Bojana with Frankish friends, and knew that there was a great water further on, associated in his mind with partings and sorrow; for whenever his companions reached its shores, they would go away from him in a big londra, never to return.

He looked very plaintively at us all the day, for he knew that the cruel old story was to be repeated.

Early in the afternoon we reached the bend in the river that had been described to us, so once more shouldered our guns and commenced our march. Our way lay across a flat country covered with a dense jungle of thorn. The road was if possible more abominable than any other we had met with during our whole journey.

It was not till late at night that we reached Dulcigno, and took up our quarters in a dirty little khan, for this port possesses no such thing as an hotel. We cooked some beef, and after a good supper retired to a hay-loft, where we were able to make ourselves very comfortable for the night.

The next morning we were able to inspect Dulcigno. A very picturesque little place it is, built at the foot of a fine valley, which opens on the sea. There is no harbour, properly speaking—merely an unprotected roadstead. We were told that the Austrian Lloyd's steamers did not touch here now, but anchored off a valley some two hours further north, where there was better shelter. When the wind blows strong on shore, the steamer cannot touch even there.

Dulcigno is a town of about 6000 inhabitants. These are for the most part Mussulmen. They have a peculiarly ferocious look, and seem to have little occupation.

Dulcigno was once a prosperous place, for many a ship was here launched and equipped for piratical purposes. Her sailors were renowned as being the bravest and most ferocious buccaneers of the Mediterranean. We have now come to look upon piracy as such an extinct profession, in the Mediterranean at least, that it seems strange to remember that it is, after all, but a few years since this was the ostensible occupation of the whole population of this coast. Many of the discontented, wild-looking fishermen we saw mending their nets on the shingle beach well remembered the good old times, and had themselves taken a part in seizing some stately Italian schooner, or bright-coloured Dalmatian felucca. We found the carrier and his string of horses just starting for the spot off which the Austrian Lloyd anchors, to unload or take on board goods for and from Scutari. As several of the horses were without burdens, we were able to ride. The road from Dulcigno to the little bay to which we were bound was across the most fertile and cultivated country we had yet seen in Albania. We passed through very forests of olives; groves of oranges covered the steep hills that sloped down to the calm Adriatic.; pretty white houses, built in the Italian style, were seen rising from the groves; and the people we met on the way had a prosperous look about them, which astonished us, and reminded us that we were approaching civilization.

At last we came on a valley whose slopes were entirely covered with olives. At the foot of this valley, the two hills that formed it projected into the sea, terminating in precipitous cliffs, thus forming a little shingle-fringed bay. This was our destination. By the shore were pitched three or four tents, where were encamped a body of soldiers—I presume, on coast-guard duty; for their officer had rather a queer discussion with Marco as to the contents of our coffin. He wished to have it opened. Marco indignantly refused to allow anything of the sort to be done. "They are Englishmen," he said. This, he thought, was a sufficient explanation. The good fellow had one definite and fixed idea, at any rate, on the subject of Englishmen. He considered that they were a worthy and eccentric people, who had no country of their own, but who, by divine right, were entitled to do exactly what they liked in any country, not being subject to any laws whatever. This idea, I have found, is shared with him by many of my travelling countrymen.

There was a shrill whistle, and the steamer suddenly appeared round the southern point.

We placed our baggage in a boat, bid adieu to

Marco, who kissed our hands over and over again, and wept to see us go; enjoined him to see Dick Deadeye safely back to Scutari—and embarked. Poor Dick Deadeye was inconsolable. It required Marco and two soldiers to hold him back from jumping into the boat after us. The wailings of the poor old dog were most pathetic.

I suppose that he is now vagabondizing about the capital once more, philosophizing on the inconstancy of human friendship. By this time, probably, he has re-attached himself to his old friends the frontier commissioners, who, I believe, were to renew their labours this May. Our general appearance, our baggage, especially the coffin with its painted lid, caused some amusement on the steamer.

I will not enter into the incidents of our return journey. For seven days we steamed along the wild coast, and among the rocky islands, till we reached Trieste, whence we took train for Calais, and so back to London. It was just after that heavy snowstorm that extended over nearly half of Europe.

From Trieste to London the whole country was deeply buried. At Venice the snow was two feet deep. In Paris all traffic had been stopped. London was little better.

And now I must bid farewell to those that have

followed me thus far; and to those that seek a tourist-unexplored, not over-inaccessible country, for a summer tour, let me strongly recommend these interesting lands of ancient Illyria.

FINIS.

www.ingramcontent.com/pod-product-compliance
Lightning Source LLC
Chambersburg PA
CBHW032045230426
43672CB00009B/1476